People Make Play

People Make Play

The impact of staffed play provision on children, families and communities

A research report written by Demos for Play England

Joost Beunderman

Play England aims for all children and young people in England to have regular access and opportunity for free, inclusive, local play provision and play space.

Play England provides advice and support to promote good practice, and works to ensure that the importance of play is recognised by policy-makers, planners and the public.

Play England is part of NCB and supported by the Big Lottery Fund.

www.playengland.org.uk

NCB's vision is a society in which all children and young people are valued and their rights are respected.

By advancing the well-being of all children and young people across every aspect of their lives, NCB aims to:

- reduce inequalities in childhood
- ensure children and young people have a strong voice in all matters that affect their lives
- promote positive images of children and young people
- enhance the health and well-being of all children and young people
- encourage positive and supportive family, and other environments.

NCB has adopted and works within the UN Convention on the Rights of the Child.

Published for Play England by NCB

National Children's Bureau, 8 Wakley Street, London EC1V 7QE
Tel: 020 7843 6000
Website: www.ncb.org.uk
Registered charity number: 258825

NCB works in partnership with Children in Scotland (www.childreninscotland.org.uk) and Children in Wales (www.childreninwales.org.uk).

Play England is part of NCB and is supported by the Big Lottery Fund.

ISBN: 978-1-905818-52-5

British Library Cataloguing in Publication Data
A catalogue record for this book is available from the British Library.

Contents

Foreword

Foreword by Richard Reeves, Director, Demos

We live in serious times. Politicians spend most of their time wearing grave expressions, as they outline plans to tackle the biggest budget deficit for two generations, or the details of the latest terrorist plot. It might seem an odd moment to make the case for play. Surely play is for children, or for less troubled times. But to neglect play is to neglect those very aspects of our humanity that we work so hard to protect and develop.

Economic growth and physical security are not ends in themselves. They are means to the end of a full, flourishing life for all our citizens. The capacity and opportunity to play – for all of us, and especially for our children – is at the heart of a good life.

The philosopher Martha Nussbaum lists the capability to play among the core capabilities necessary for human development. This is seen by many as a controversial item on her list, and there is no doubt that it is hard to measure capabilities for play. But Nussbaum is onto something very important. The blend of imagination, courage and collaboration necessary for play captures something essential about the human condition. Demos has a long-standing and deep interest in issues around play, and the playfulness that characterises a good life, and a good society. In this sense, play is the most serious business of all.

Foreword by Adrian Voce, Director, Play England

The notion of 'playworkers', on the face of it, seems counter intuitive.

Even for some researchers, the relevance of the adult in play is not always apparent, particularly for children beyond the early years. Playing is deeply instinctive, following its own innate course, determined and directed by the child. What does it have to do with adults, let alone workers? Indeed, isn't this a contradiction in terms?

What this timely report by Demos illustrates is that, in the modern world, adults have a vital role, not in the actual play of children but in the provision of the physical and social space that it needs. A wide range of settings for all ages of children and young people – including many parts of the public realm that were once rich play domains but are now increasingly proscribed to children – need the presence of responsible adults with an understanding of play, if we are to reverse the trend of recent decades and return to children the freedom of the outdoor world. A variety of indicators suggest that we cannot afford to fail.

The playworker, as such, is a comparatively recent development. The role first took shape in the 1950s when inner city children – increasingly squeezed out of common public space by planners, traffic and changing attitudes to children, and a long way from the wild and green space that is the natural environment for outdoor play – had taken to first exploring and then colonising old bomb sites and demolished housing blocks, turning them into ad hoc playgrounds by erecting their own ramshackle structures and dens from whatever scrap materials they could lay their hands on. These places offered countless opportunities for playing of the kind that children instinctively seek out. Moulding and manipulating the environment to suit the game – from erecting a tent with a blanket between two chairs, to damning a stream in the woods – is a fundamental part of children's play; as is the thrill of creative possibility and the interchange between mastery and uncertainty that all children experience as they invent and continually reinvent their own play worlds.

The waste grounds of the decaying urban landscape of post-war Britain offered an abundance of such adventures. But they were often hazardous and insecure; and rarely supervised. Adult volunteers got involved initially to make them safer without losing their unique sense of adventure. Over time this new pact between children and adults for play, developed its own unique architecture of self-built structures using old telegraph poles, scaffolding planks, tyres and ropes, allowing children to clamber, run, climb and swing to heights and over distances never dreamed of on the swings and roundabouts of municipal playgrounds.

This partnership didn't just allow children to build the playgrounds of their imaginations; it also helped them to develop boundaries and rules, to secure more resources. The sites and their ethos were able to develop and evolve. They became socially more inclusive, so that younger children, girls, disabled children and those from minority communities could feel as much at home as the older boys who would otherwise dominate. A wider range of activities became possible: sand, water and fire play were the norm, while all manner of scrap materials and countless other 'loose parts' would be commandeered solely for the purpose of children having the fullest range of play opportunities. These spaces thus became unique communities of children and adults, cooperating to create not just physical, but social and cultural environments dedicated solely to children doing their own thing in their own way.

The richness of experience derived by the adult volunteers and, increasingly, paid staff on adventure playgrounds inspired many of them to see it as a vocation and they gradually came to identify themselves as 'playworkers'. Local parents and community leaders often took on responsibility for the planning, campaigning, fundraising and management that enabled the playgrounds to employ them.

Playwork provides rich opportunities to study children's play and this emerging profession developed its own body of work, drawing on the different sciences of play but adding to it from the unique perspective afforded to the observant practitioner. As well as increasing our understanding of play, what these studies and their emerging theories also did was describe and define the role of the playworker. These eventually became formalised within occupational principles and standards to underpin recognised training and qualifications. Trained playworkers are now to be found in after-school clubs, play centres and holiday schemes, as well as adventure playgrounds, up and down the country.

Playwork is complementary but outside what is sometimes called 'the education continuum', and is no less important. Because children will play anywhere, playwork can be applied to a wider range of settings than formal children's services. Increasingly, as this report shows, playworkers are employed to good effect, not on defined sites at all, but within wider public spaces. Where playworkers originally helped children to colonise disused bombsites for play, play rangers are now helping them to turn whole parks and other open spaces into potential playgrounds.

Not that the original adventure playground is outdated. For children in dense urban or suburban areas where playing in open space is simply not an option, staffed adventure playgrounds are still the best response. The government's play pathfinder programme, supported by Play England, will see at least 30 new ones built by 2011.

In today's Britain, a typical 8- to 10-year-old is effectively battery-reared compared to the free-range childhoods enjoyed by his or her parents and grandparents; spending five or more hours a day in front of a screen, driven everywhere and rarely, if ever, allowed out without an adult. Obesity, rickets, attention deficit disorder and anti-social behaviour are just some of the symptoms of an increasingly sedentary child population, as more and more children are denied the fundamental expression of their energy and vitality through play.

The main political parties agree that children's lack of space and opportunity for outdoor play is a serious problem needing a proportionate policy response. The Conservatives' Childhood Review, *More Ball Games* called for more supervision of public space for play, echoing the Demos report commissioned by Play England in 2007, that children should be 'seen and heard' as part of community life.

Meanwhile the government's Children's Plan included a ten-year Play Strategy with the aim of ensuring that, by 2020, in 'every residential area there are a variety of places for play, free of charge, supervised and unsupervised' with children and young people having a clear, respected 'stake in public space'. The strategy includes training for playworkers and a cross-professional programme for planners, social housing managers, police and others, to work together towards the vision of a child-friendly, playable public realm.

£235m of mainly capital funding underpins the first three years of the Play Strategy and will produce 3500 unstaffed play spaces by 2011. The challenge now is to ensure that future revenue funding is directed to employing the staff and supporting the volunteers – 'the software of play provision', as characterised by this report – that will be needed to ensure these physical spaces (the hardware) are well used, and to make the wider 2020 vision a reality.

Playwork has come a long way since the days of the early adventure playgrounds. This report demonstrates its enduring value to children, families and whole communities and shines a light on the way ahead.

Acknowledgements

The author and Play England gratefully acknowledge the time and input of Issy Cole-Hamilton (Play England), of the Sounding Board group members (Steven Chown, Stuart Douglas, Perry Else, Tim Ferguson, Andy Furze, Mark Gladwin, Haki Kapasi, Warren Koehler, Frank O'Malley, Wendy Russell and Alan Sutton) and of the external experts, Marc Armitage and Morgan Leichter-Saxby, who provided invaluable expertise at different stages of the project. We are also indebted to Tania Tam for providing methodological support; and to our excellent interns Nicola Hughes, Talia Brun Marcen and Felicity Meerloo for their work throughout. Lastly, we are grateful for the kind and enthusiastic assistance we received from the staff in our six case studies.

Executive summary

People Make Play provides a range of qualitative perspectives on the role and potential impact of good quality, staffed, local play provision in the lives of children and young people, their parents and the wider community. The aim was to provide insight into how the beneficial impact could be captured and communicated to relevant audiences. The research focused on play provision for children aged between 8 and 13 years, and on staffed provision alone: the study did not look at any unsupervised provision. The project was commissioned by Play England.

The research draws on recent literature reviews about the importance of unstructured play to children's lives, and is based on six in-depth case studies of good quality, free, staffed play provision across England. These were:

- Gainsborough Adventure Playground Association, Gainsborough, Lincolnshire
- Glamis Adventure Playground, London Borough of Tower Hamlets
- Wansdyke Play Association's play ranger project in Radstock, Bath and North East Somerset
- Reccy Rangers, Cambridge City Council's Children and Young People Participation Service
- Newbald Church Rooms Young People's Project – East Riding of Yorkshire
- Wythenshawe Community Initiative in Manchester.

Observations and semi-structured interviews were used to draw out accounts of the different types of benefit created and experienced, as seen through the eyes of the key groups involved: children and young people themselves, parents, play staff and key policy stakeholders.

Key findings

1   Physical settings

Staffed play provision takes place in a wide variety of physical settings designed to suit the needs and opportunities of different places across the country, from a shoehorn site in a dense urban neighbourhood to a former school building in a small Yorkshire village. In practice, the successful examples studied in this research have characteristics that cut across different provision types – such as play rangers, play centres and adventure playgrounds. But however large the differences across the case studies – in history, present size, resources and organisation – they all succeed in one thing:

creating spaces for children. The presence of playworkers or play rangers in these places provides safety and increases the confidence of children to play freely, as well as increasing the range of play opportunities within the space provided. To children and parents this provides a marked contrast with the wider public realm, which all too often fails to provide the same safety and diversity of opportunity.

2   Children's stories

The stories of the children in this report demonstrate that, while they love well-designed playgrounds and attractive, spacious play areas, it is the staff – the 'software' – rather than the 'hardware' of play equipment that, for them, really makes the difference. They enjoy the freedom to play in their own way that playworkers and play rangers give them, but what also shines through is the confidence that they derive from supportive, responsible adults: to play games, take risks, test boundaries and socialise with others in a way that is not always possible at home, on the street, at school or in unsupervised playgrounds.

Staffed play provision often takes place where children may have difficult and complex lives, and where the wider public realm is generally inhospitable to them. Providing a place to roam free, a safe haven in a hostile world, these sites have real value as places where children can be themselves, have unique and cherished experiences, bond with their peers and associate with older and younger children too.

Trusted, personal relationships with adults are highly valuable for children and young people; and less common, in our atomised and cautious society, than they used to be. In the settings explored here, these adult-child relationships are of a different kind from those that they usually experience at home or in school.

Children's active involvement in designing, making decisions and then, literally, building, together with the staff, the kind of play-scapes that inspire them is just the most tangible evidence of a relationship that is more of a partnership than anything else. Equally important is the time afforded to them by a friendly grown-up who wants nothing of them but for them to be themselves.

3   Staff stories

The experiences of the children at these sites are not, of course, unconnected from the approach of those who staff them. Six of our case study settings share a set of fundamental values, rooted in the principles that underpin playwork training and practice. Within these Playwork Principles (see page 2), the role of the adult is to support and facilitate the play process in all its richness and complexity, rather than to direct or steer what children do. Our playworkers gently help to shape both the physical and the social environment to offer all children the fullest possibility to play. Children playing can be boisterous, cruel, sometimes violent. The staff see their role as striking a balance between allowing full expression through play and cultivating an atmosphere of safety, tolerance and mutual respect, intervening carefully only where necessary to ensure that the sites are inclusive to all. Much of the success in the cases studied is underpinned by such efforts, as well as through outreach work with under-represented groups.

Within our case studies, playworkers see their work not as isolated from neighbourhoods and communities but as connected to the wider context of their locality. They increasingly work beyond the boundaries of their site to explore and expand play opportunities, thereby changing the culture and possibilities within the public realm at large. In this respect, play providers are at the forefront of public services innovation.

4 Making a difference in children's lives

Children, young people, parents and staff have many stories to tell about how play provision has had an impact on their lives. Children mention many elements of 'learning' as a natural aspect of the play experience, and how this is about 'learning to play' and to be inventive, confident and social, which they hold as equally important to learning practical things in school. They talk about their experience in terms of trajectories of progress: about overcoming initial difficulties, whether social or physical, about taking new risks and sharing stories with others. There is a huge range of life skills and attitudes that children say they obtain as part of this process: from caring, sharing and being kind, to standing up for oneself or asking for help. These experiences, it would seem, can change children's perception of their neighbourhood, transforming it into a trusted place in which they feel welcome, know their peers and others, and consider themselves at home. In other words, providing 'somewhere to go, something to do' has an impact on these youngsters' positive perception of the places where they live. Parents and others involved – staff and other stakeholders – confirm such indications that play provision contributes to a growth in what Amartya Sen and Martha Nussbaum (Sen 1979, Nussbaum and Sen 1993) have called 'capabilities' – the positive freedoms needed for each human being to live a fulfilling life.

5   Parents' stories

Parents and carers are frequently big supporters of staffed play provision. Across our case studies, they have been eager to share powerful stories of how it has changed the lives of their children, of themselves as parents, and how it has benefitted their neighbourhoods as places to live. They recognise that staffed play provision is a crucial ingredient of their children's lives – an integral experience that their children would otherwise sorely miss. They are also keenly aware of the mix of learning, socialising and health benefits that children gain from playing, but primarily emphasise how their children gain precious and unique experiences when play is allowed to take place for its own sake.

But these sites make a difference in parents' lives too. They bring parents into contact with other parents and facilitate the creation of informal social bonds and support networks – crucial lifelines in deprived neighbourhoods and for parents in need. In fact, parents feel that play provision can transform their communities, by cutting across social divides, bringing neighbours into contact with each other and creating a greater sense of community. Support is often expressed through volunteering, which in turn can be beneficial to parents, who learn valuable skills. In other words, play provision can increase local social capital where it is needed most. Because of all this, many parents feel that the value of these play settings, as expressed by what their children tell them or what they experience themselves, can be equal to or higher than many services for which they have to pay – including childcare, school trips or sports activities. Moreover, they realise that all this cannot be taken for granted: in some cases, the presence of good quality play provision has even served as a deciding factor in whether to move to or stay in a neighbourhood.

6   Policy partners' responses

The importance of play is increasingly being recognised by policy-makers and public service stakeholders. This is for a mix of intrinsic and instrumental reasons: whilst first and foremost recognising children's right to good play provision, these stakeholders also recognise the difference that play provision can make to other outcomes for children and their own professional objectives. In this context, they also understand the crucial role of staff in expanding play opportunities and in actualising and intensifying these benefits.

Across the public and voluntary sectors engaged in this research, there is a keen understanding that such benefits need to be captured and communicated in order to ensure that staffed play provision is accountable, legitimate and sustainable. However, there is no single way of doing this – whilst measuring quantitative outcomes is seen as valuable by some, others emphasise the need to improve output data (attendance and uptake); and others see the untapped potential of qualitative narratives such as, for example, communicating the children's own stories.

7 Institutional links

A wide range of institutional links are evident in the daily practice of successful play providers. Local schools, children's services, parks staff, family support workers, libraries, police and elected members are just some examples found of play professionals having regular contact with a wider network of support for children and families.

Because play provision is often in areas of high deprivation, and because its ethos of enabling self-directed, freely chosen activity makes it more accessible to children otherwise at risk of exclusion, it can often build important bridges between the statutory children's services and so called hard-to-reach children and families. There are plenty of examples here of the way staffed play settings are increasingly seen as a vital element of the multi-agency, integrated services approach that is central to sustained, improved outcomes for children.

Firstly, far from simple recreational space, staffed play provision is effectively a holistic service to children and young people. Informal counselling, mentoring and coaching along with advice on drugs, sex and staying safe are all part and parcel of the playworker's role, together with the all important sign-posting and referral to statutory services, including local safeguarding boards. They can also be a gateway to sports, arts and other cultural opportunities. In this way staffed play provision can be seen to fill a vital gap for the middle years, between statutory early education and youth provision.

Secondly, these places are touch points for children and young people's engagement with their physical and social environments. Being places they elect – rather than being referred or compelled – to attend, they serve to enhance children's sense of place and community. Their relations with both peers and the adult world improve, as does their respect for the public realm, enabling them to belong and to make more positive contributions to their area. Thirdly, these settings often provide a focus for volunteering, sharing local knowledge and other resources with the wider voluntary and community sector. Being located where children are, and want to be, they are thus regarded as cornerstones for community involvement.

Finally, the huge added value of volunteers and voluntary management committees, the resourcefulness and self-sufficiency of the playwork ethos (adventure playgrounds and their scrap store suppliers were the original recyclers) and their refreshing lack of bureaucratic administrative tiers, make a significant economic case for this form of provision. Any cost-benefit analysis of the projects highlighted here would surely demonstrate high returns compared to the more established statutory services.

Playworkers are rightly cautious of their unique service becoming instrumental to other agendas. But recognising their important role in integrated local services and the additional benefits this brings to children and families should not undermine their primary purpose. Indeed, it is because they exist solely to support free play that makes them so valuable. And their networking has the additional benefit of promoting a wider understanding of children's play and its importance throughout the public realm, and within the professions that shape it.

People Make Play: Conclusions

The research in this study shows how successful staffed play provision make a significant difference to children, parents and neighbourhoods. First and foremost, it extends and diversifies the opportunities for children to play by unlocking the potential of public spaces and giving children and parents the confidence to use them. The study also demonstrates that staffed provision can be integral to the broader network of support for children and families to live better lives, achieve more positive outcomes and belong, in a very real sense, to a thriving local community.

The present time holds both opportunity and risk for this kind of provision. The Children's Plan and subsequent Play Strategy, following on from a significant injection of lottery funding, brought unprecedented national investment into this non-statutory part of the children's sector. Politicians and other influencers have regularly spoken of the importance of active outdoor play, and the barriers to accessing it that today's children face. The case for the benefits of dedicated play provision appears to have been made.

What this research demonstrates is that some of the best opportunities for the children most in need do not come about from investment purely in the 'hardware' of sites and equipment, but through the understanding, skills and commitment of dedicated staff and volunteers. Playworkers and play rangers turn physical spaces into places of opportunity, imagination and belonging. For many children in many places, investing in hardware will never be enough. The best opportunities to play are shaped by **people** – the 'software' of play.

As local areas seek to embed the recent changes and sustain the growth of opportunity for children and families, local authority members, commissioners and managers must unlock revenue resources to enable the maintenance and growth of staffed play provision where it is most needed.

Policy recommendations

Sustaining and more widely replicating the kind of provision showcased here will require – from a range of agencies across different sectors – better communication, more support and further funding.

Better communication

To make the case for the sustainable growth of staffed play provision, with the ongoing application of revenue resources, the government, local authorities, play providers and advocates like Play England need to communicate clearly – to the public and to policy influencers – the full benefits of staffed play provision. The experience of the culture and arts sector, for example, shows that recognising the instrumental benefits of something need not undermine belief in its intrinsic value.

Play providers need to strengthen the way they communicate and work with local communities. This implies finding creative ways to capture and explain their ethos and work; tracking more carefully how many children they reach; widening their appeal to under-represented groups; working in the wider public realm as well as within their sites; and working together with other third sector and public bodies. The case studies in this research are successful partly because they have understood this challenge – the sector at large would benefit from following their lead.

More support

Play England and other organisations in the sector should recognise that improving communication will be a challenge for many organisations, and should work with local authorities to build upon and improve the support infrastructure and organisational capacity for play providers that should now be possible from the legacy of the lottery initiative and the support put in place to underpin the Play Strategy.

For staffed play providers to communicate their work confidently to the public implies supporting and resourcing playworkers and their agencies to talk about what they know and love – the incredible stories of children at play – and enabling a better sharing of good practice and relationship-building across the sector

Further funding

Government and local authorities should ensure that the new investment in the 'hardware' of sites and equipment is followed up and sustained by appropriate support for the 'software' of play: the staff and volunteers that can realise its potential for children and families. Funding programmes and commissioning strategies should reflect this.

Equally, new investment should pay closer attention to the success of existing provision. Important as capital investment in play provision is, funders and commissioners should seek now to strengthen the long-term sustainability of local 'play offers'. This means supporting valuable local projects like those illustrated here, and to invest more widely in the most important play resource of all: the people who make play.

Introduction

Demos was commissioned by Play England to undertake a detailed social analysis of the role and potential impact of good quality, staffed, local play provision on the lives of children and young people, their parents and the wider community. This research focuses on children's play for those aged between 8 and 13 years. The key aim was to provide insight into how the beneficial impact of play provision can be captured and communicated to relevant audiences.

This report gives an overview and analysis of the research, which focused on qualitative accounts of the different types of benefit created and experienced as seen through the eyes of the key parties: children and young people themselves, parents, play provision staff and key policy stakeholders. The research was carried out across six case studies, chosen as examples of good quality, staffed play provision across a range of settings. Also included is an overview of key strands in the relevant literature; key issues to consider for a possible next, quantitative phase; and conclusions and recommendations to the play sector arising from the research so far.

The word 'play' in this report is used in the sense defined in the *Charter for Children's Play* (Play England 2007) as:

> Play is what children do when they follow their own ideas and interests, in their own way and for their own reasons. These activities are freely chosen, personally directed and may take place with or without adult involvement. They may take place in the home; the street, the local community or on school premises, including the playground, and the countryside. Such activities may be undertaken by the child on their own or with peers.

Playwork

The *Charter for Children's Play* states that 'Children's play is enriched by skilled playworkers.' Playwork is essentially an approach to working with children in which they determine and control the content and intent of their play, rather than it being led or directed. Engaging in play is seen as a beneficial outcome in itself as well as contributing to other outcomes. It is a process through which children make sense of their world and their place in it, without the need for an end result or product.

The play process for children includes exploration, trying out things, testing boundaries of ability as they grow, learning from successes and mistakes to build resilience and adaptability.

In other words, children are the experts in their play, and are very clear about how play contributes to their overall well-being, happiness and ability to be with friends and meet new ones, to stay healthy and fit, enjoy their local area and feel safe while enjoying new challenges.

The government's national Play Strategy supports this approach: its first principle says that children need to enjoy their childhood as well as grow up prepared for adult life.

From time to time children may need the support of skilled playworkers to extend their play, the range of places they feel safe to play in, or to ensure they don't harm themselves or others. Playworkers understand and apply the need for a 'high response, low intervention' style of working, where their response is based on observation and reflective practice and any intervention is only to support the play.

Playwork Principles

Developed by the play sector as fundamental statements about the relationship between children's play and playwork, the Playwork Principles are held in trust by the Playwork Principles Scrutiny Group. They have been endorsed by SkillsActive and underpin the National Occupational Standards for playwork training and qualifications.

The full text is reproduced below.

These principles establish the professional and ethical framework for playwork and as such must be regarded as a whole. They describe what is unique about play and playwork, and provide the playwork perspective for working with children and young people. They are based on the recognition that children and young people's capacity for positive development will be enhanced if given access to the broadest range of environments and play opportunities.

1. All children and young people need to play. The impulse to play is innate. Play is a biological, psychological and social necessity, and is fundamental to the healthy development and well-being of individuals and communities.
2. Play is a process that is freely chosen, personally directed and intrinsically motivated. That is, children and young people determine and control the content and intent of their play, by following their own instincts, ideas and interests, in their own way for their own reasons.
3. The prime focus and essence of playwork is to support and facilitate the play process and this should inform the development of play policy, strategy, training and education.
4. For playworkers, the play process takes precedence and playworkers act as advocates for play when engaging with adult-led agendas.
5. The role of the playworker is to support all children and young people in the creation of a space in which they can play.
6. The playworker's response to children and young people playing is based on a sound up-to-date knowledge of the play process, and reflective practice.
7. Playworkers recognise their own impact on the play space and also the impact of children and young people's play on the playworker.
8. Playworkers choose an intervention style that enables children and young people to extend their play. All playworker intervention must balance risk with the developmental benefit and well-being of children.

1 Literature review

Image: Newbald Church Rooms Young People's Project

This literature review aims to give an overview of different assessments that have been made of the impact of play and play provision, and link these to a set of wider, currently relevant, policy fields.

The review does not seek to make a comprehensive or wider argument regarding the beneficial impact of play in general. The value and benefits of play have been the subject of intensive research over past decades and there is ample evidence, from a wide range of sources, that children who have the opportunity to play freely benefit from it in a large number of ways. Those benefits cover the very foundations of their bodily and mental development, their health, emotional development and resilience, creativity and problem-solving skills, socialisation amongst peers and the sense of agency and opportunities they have to influence change in their everyday environment (for examples see: Cole-Hamilton and Gill 2002; Cole-Hamilton and others 2002; Beunderman, Hannon and Bradwell 2007; Brown 2006; New Policy Institute 2002; Children's Play Council, National Playing Fields Association and Playlink 2000; Lester and Russell 2008; Coalter and Taylor

2001). Instead, this review will focus on the different ways in which researchers have tried to capture such impact.

Most empirical research tends to focus on the specific benefits of play and play provision within certain broad fields – its impact on early years development, health, educational results and anti-social behaviour. It is not surprising therefore that the methodologies used are highly specific to the fields chosen – from clinical trial-like approaches focusing on long-term measurable effects to qualitative surveys asking for perception and opinion (Santer, Griffiths and Goodall 2007). Below we highlight a representative series of different approaches although, as early years development falls outside this study, we do not discuss them here.

Benefits of play

Several researchers and policy-makers have identified a number of conceptual and methodological problems associated with attempts to establish the benefits of play outside of a deprivation model (Barnett 1990; Children's Play Council, National Playing Fields Association and Playlink 2000). These are, primarily, the difficulties of defining 'play' in a variety of social and spatial contexts; the complex models required to examine causal relationships; the difficulties inherent in longitudinal studies without clear control groups; and changes in the definitions and functions of 'play' as young people develop. Nonetheless, a number of attempts have been made to 'quantify the unquantifiable', some of which we examine below.

Health

In the field of health, there have been ample studies to show that activity level patterns, including sport, are set early in life (Kuh and Cooper 1992, Perkins and others 2004). Current widespread concern over the low levels of physical exercise among British children and the general decline in physical fitness and health has at times over-emphasised the exertive value of play, which is predicated on a very narrow notion of what play is (Cale and Almond 1992, McKendrick, Fielder and Bradford 1999, British Heart Foundation 2000). An interesting approach, however, has been the measuring of activity levels with regard to different play settings: Mackett's 2004 study of activity levels is useful for supporting the case for the benefits of **unstructured play** on health. Children were fitted with portable motion sensors and they kept activity and travel diaries. The sensors produce results in terms of activity calories (the calories consumed in carrying out events as opposed to the calories consumed in maintaining bodily functions). It was found that whilst physical education lessons and structured games generate the most intensive physical activity, unstructured ball games, walking and playing are not far behind. From these results, conclusions have been drawn about the impact of children's activity patterns and travel behaviour on their overall quantity of physical activity (Mackett 2004).

Mental health

In terms of children's mental health, one short-term study provides evidence that play can help reduce levels of anxiety in children (Barnett and Storm 1981). Equally, the 2007 Fact Sheet produced by the Children Youth and Environments Center for Research and Design shows ample evidence that being able to access natural areas in which to play has significant benefits. This is related to play therapy, although a distinction must be drawn between this and free play which may, at times and under the child's own direction, also be understood to have therapeutic qualities (Sturrock and Else 1998).

Improved learning

In the field of education, there is observational evidence from teachers to support the idea that play contributes to better learning. For example, Caseberry suggested in 1998, following a Playlink Play at School project, that: 'The opportunities which playtime is providing are helping to develop skills – physical, language and social – and attitudes – concentration, tolerance, perseverance – in the children, and these are enhancing their ability to learn in more formal settings within the classroom' (Children's Play Council, National Playing Fields Association and Playlink 2000: 10). Of particular note are the Effective Provision of Pre-School Education (EPPE) studies, longitudinal studies funded by the Department for Children, Schools and Families (DCSF), which can be found on the Institute of Education website. The studies focus on the progress and development of 3,000 children from pre-school to the end of Key Stage 3 in secondary school (ages 3 to 14), including investigations in the different settings where learning can take place – including play environments. However, the directive involvement by adults in children's play and the supposed negative impact this has on the development of creativity has been researched in the United States. Studies show that the attempts of adults to direct play towards educational ambitions was in fact detrimental to children's direct learning processes (*Independent* 13 June 2000).

Community cohesion

As regards socialisation, the report *Making Playful Learning Visible* studied 66 parents and carers observing their children's play over four months (Thomas and Bradburne 2006). They noted how much their children learn through play, and how they, in turn, could use this in day-to-day parenting techniques. Data was collected through self-reported pre- and post-session questionnaires, group discussions, face-to-face interviews, observations and field notes, although not all instruments were used in all settings. This strongly suggests how play enhances community bonds and learning for parents, supporting assertions made in *Best Play* (Children's Play Council, National Playing Fields Association and Playlink 2000) that play provision can provide a means of promoting social cohesion, tackling social exclusion and providing a focus for informal networks by offering a place in which children can play and feel safe. This becomes even more important as it has been demonstrated that those children most in need (children from some ethnic minority groups and those with disabilities, for example) are those who suffer the greatest restrictions on access.

Improved understanding of environment

A Demos/Green Alliance study, *A Child's Place*, used 'a series of interviews with children around the UK, aged ten to eleven, to establish their attitudes towards their environment and how this affects them' (Thomas and Thompson 2004: 3) and found amongst other things that children gained their best understanding of the environment through their own exploration of the natural world. This was harder for children in urban areas who had poor levels of access.

In general, this review corroborates the assertion made in the New Policy Institute's 2002 literature review that 'much of the material is of a qualitative nature rather than quantitative' and that it is therefore of a descriptive nature, more successful in arguing the **types** of benefits that play brings, rather than the **scale** of those benefits.

Such arguments have been powerful in linking play provision to a series of policy issues that are currently high on the government agenda.

Policy

This is, primarily, the Every Child Matters agenda and its five core outcomes – be healthy, stay safe, enjoy and achieve, make a positive contribution and achieve economic well-being. It is now widely recognised that play impacts – directly or indirectly – on all of these five outcomes (DCSF 2008, Lester and Russell 2008).

Equally, play provision could impact on other policy areas – such as those of the Department of Communities and Local Government (CLG), which coordinates policies on neighbourhood renewal and open space improvements: 'Our vision is for a renaissance of England's green spaces, so that by 2008 the majority of local areas in England have at least one quality green space – with a Green Flag Award to prove it – and over 75 per cent of people are satisfied with their green spaces' (see the CLG website for details). The Cleaner Safer Greener programme is a joint initiative requiring partnership and ongoing consultation to create a climate of best practice but is directed by CLG (see its website for details). The links between neighbourhood renewal programmes and play are further explored in *Fair Play* (DCSF 2008).

Further, the Office for the Third Sector aims to develop and support an environment that enables the third sector to thrive, increasing its contribution to Britain's society, economy and environment. Working in partnership with central and local government, one of its overall aims is to 'strengthen communities, drawing together people from different sections of society'. An example is Volunteering for All, a two-year programme worth £3 million. The programme was launched in September 2006 and ran until March 2009, its aim being to identify and tackle barriers to volunteering (see the Office for the Third Sector website for details). In the national Play Strategy, the importance of volunteering to play and the multiple benefits this can bring are recognised and built upon (DCSF 2008).

The government's consultation document on the national Play Strategy also explicitly refers to the new National Indicator Set that measures local authorities' performance on national policy priorities (details available on the CLG website, accessed 20 October 2008). It states that:

> There are a number of other indicators in the National Indicator Set where a focus on play could help with delivery. For example, active play will be a significant contributor to the delivery of the two indicators on child obesity, which are central to tackling that issue. Play in communities can also support public satisfaction with local areas (DCSF 2008: 52).

In local implementation strategies, the contribution of play to not just health and socialisation but to community cohesion is now generally taken for granted. *Fair Play* (DCSF 2008) recognises this, as does Greater London Authority's 2008 planning guidance, which, for example, states that play facilities are therefore 'a key component of an exemplary sustainable world city' (GLA 2007).

The cost of inactivity

The benefits of play provision have been linked to economic advantage, but such analysis is still rather rare, due either to lack of data or hesitation about the instrumentalisation of play. Where such links are made, this happens primarily through inferring costs to the state, for example the cost of healthcare later in life (an indirect benefit) or the cost of vandalism and anti-social behaviour (sometimes measured as a direct benefit). Derived benefits are valid, but their indirect nature means that a series of assumptions need to be made regarding the pricing and discounting of key variables such as health and educational attainment. These are inherently open for discussion and contestation; an 'objective' way of doing cost–benefit analysis does not exist (Atkinson and others 2006).

In 2004 the Department of Health estimated the financial cost of inactivity in England to be £8.2 billion annually – including the rising costs of treating chronic diseases such as coronary heart disease and diabetes. The contribution of inactivity to obesity is estimated to cost a further £2.5 billion each year (Department of Health 2004). Current estimates are that two-thirds of adults and a third of all children are overweight or obese, and that this will rise to nine-tenths of adults and two-thirds of children should trends continue to 2050; the cost is estimated at £50 billion per year (Department of Health 2008, Foresight 2007).

Projects examined by the Thames Valley Police showed significant reductions in vandalism and petty crime following the installation of play facilities and a youth shelter. Their evidence is based on case studies such as Marcham in Oxfordshire where after a new shelter was built, Thames Valley Police found reduced 'problems of anti-social behaviour'. In Banbury in Oxfordshire, the cost of repairs to young children's play equipment dropped by 25 per cent (£10,000) in the first year after installing youth recreation facilities. In Burnley in Lancashire, a youth shelter was built in response to complaints about anti-social behaviour, after which reports of nuisance behaviour dropped by 29 per cent (across the whole town) and 50 per cent (near the park). Vandalism to play equipment dropped 87 per cent (from £580 to £70). At Aylesbury in Buckinghamshire, the cost of repairs to equipment dropped dramatically in some areas (Thames Valley Police 1999).

The fact that the costs of anti-social behaviour and crime and health costs can be measured enhances the risk of only using these to measure the value of play provision. When it comes to costs to the state, such relatively easy-to-measure variables often tend to eclipse more complex value judgements, leading to narrow concepts of cost-efficiency being valued over other considerations. Even more fundamentally, those things that are easy to measure tend to become objectives, whilst those that are hard to measure are downplayed or ignored. Hence, within public policy-making, discussions about value concepts have focused on ways to capture what matters to the public rather than focusing only on improvements in efficiency. This concept – public value – has led the way towards a different approach to value interpretations (Kelly and others 2002).

However, it is debatable if even such a widened concept of public value does justice to play provision: the value of play provision to the public might still be an instrumentalised interpretation of something that is as much about enjoyment in the here and now as it is about children's development into adulthood and their nation's future. Whenever play is seen primarily as a vehicle for a wider social and economic agenda, there will be what Stuart Lester and Wendy Russell call a 'tension field' between the policy context, the literature on intrinsic benefits and the daily practice of playwork (Lester and Russell 2008). Whilst such arguments do not deny that instrumental benefits might occur, they warn against privileging these over the intrinsic enjoyment derived from play, namely the enjoyment of everyday life and having a good childhood now. They also warn against the impact this might have on the actual provision itself – it could lead adults to 'intervene in play to ensure that children play in ways that are "productive and socialising", thereby affecting the sector in its practices' (Lester and Russell 2008: 1). After all, while such value assertions might be true, and few would question the wider social benefit as a desirable outcome – is that the central purpose of play?

The risks entailed in such an approach are evident when we look at discussions in other fields which have evaluated the impact of public sector provision. A good example is the cultural sector, which deals with a concept the definition of which might be even harder to capture than 'play'. In the 1980s, culture began increasingly to be seen as the 'handmaiden' of other public policy objectives, notably economic development. Whilst in the late 1990s the new government emphasised its commitment to supporting culture for its own sake, it added a series of social objectives. As a result, meeting targets set by funders has now become a major issue for cultural leaders, leading to what John Holden has called 'a closed and ill-tempered conversation between professionals and politicians' and a crisis of legitimacy (Holden 2004). Instead, he proposes an evaluation of value that emphasises the intrinsic value of culture alongside its instrumental and institutional values (see The 'value triangle', page 76).

Crucial to this value triangle is the realisation that, without intrinsic value, no other value will be generated at all. And as such, intrinsic value can't always – and shouldn't – be measured or quantified. It moreover explains that these values play out – are created and 'consumed' – within a triangular relationship between cultural professionals, politicians and policy-makers, and the public. Chapter 5 will discuss this work, and its potential application in the play sector, in more detail.

Investment in play

As Lester and Russell (2008) observe, the government has offered an alternative to overly instrumental perceptions of play by acknowledging that play is fundamental to children's enjoyment of their lives. The Children's Plan, published in 2007, sets out governmental priorities and commitments for children's policy over the next few years (DCSF 2007). Along with announcements for significant investment in play provision, including staffed play provision, and the announcement of a national play strategy, the document explicitly recognises the intrinsic value of play, separate from its benefits on issues such as health and educational attainment.

The draft national Play Strategy *Fair Play* is built on the Children's Plan and is intended to concretise this commitment and embed policies further across government (DCSF 2008). Moreover, the government has announced that, from April 2009, the National Indicator Set will include an indicator on what children think about the parks and play areas in their local area (see the CLG website for details, accessed 20 October 2008). Significantly, this information is collected by asking children and young people directly, via the TellUs Survey.

This might suggest that, rather than outcomes, output is a key relevant factor: if we accept that play has beneficial effects and is relevant in and of itself, then the key variable is increased access. This implies that, as Lester and Russell (2008) put it, play provision should be judged on whether it enables children to play rather than on more instrumental outcomes.

A good example of such an approach is the *Evaluation of the Tower Hamlets Community Play Programme* (Creegan and others 2004). Tower Hamlets and Barnardo's conducted a survey of the impact of play provision in the area – this was mainly qualitative in nature but did use some quantitative methods of gathering and analysing data as well. In-depth, semi-structured interviews were conducted with playworkers and methods were chosen that enabled data collection from as many parents as possible given the resources available, including the use of interpreters. This included individual face-to-face and telephone interviews, group interviews and the use of a short questionnaire that included both open and closed questions. Data was collected from a total of 50 parents from eight of the ten projects. The data from children was considered the most important, although there was a focus on keeping interference minimal and fun. Methods were tailored to children's needs: drawing maps of the play area (to gauge ownership); giving guided tours; a diary/ comments book; questionnaires; writing and drawing exercises; Post-it note and disposable camera exercises; and participant observation. The ten core effects measured, based on the seven objectives of play provision described in *Best Play: What play provision should do for children* and the programme funding objectives, were:

Play Provision Objective 1 — To provide opportunities for creative, stimulating, age-appropriate play.

Play Provision Objective 2 — To enable children to exercise choice and control over their play.

Play Provision Objective 3 — To enable children to test boundaries.

Play Provision Objective 4 — To achieve an appropriate balance between risk and safety.

Service Delivery Objective 1 — To promote and provide services to both new and existing users.

Service Delivery Objective 2 — To promote and provide inclusive services which recognise diversity.

Service Delivery Objective 3 — To actively involve children and parents in service planning and delivery.

Children's Well-being Objective 1 — Children feel more confident and independent.

Children's Well-being Objective 2 — Children have increased respect for others.

Children's Well-being Objective 3 — Children's healthy growth and development are promoted.

In other words, these objectives focus primarily on the intrinsic benefits of play to children and young people, and on how provision enables a range of play opportunities, as well as focusing on its outcomes. It did not involve measuring any monetary outcome. The Barnardo's report also warns that, whilst play provision and service delivery can be evaluated in the short term, evaluating outcomes in relation to children's well-being requires a longer term approach (Creegan and others 2004: 68).

Such longer term approaches are needed in most project evaluations, not only for abstract outcome assessment. Similar techniques, of course, are used widely to evaluate the success of particular policy interventions. Two relevant examples follow:

Sport England undertook an evaluation of Sport Action Zones (Sport England 2006). Ipsos MORI were commissioned to conduct robust quantitative research including two waves of around 1,000 interviews in each selected zone. The results were compared to identify changes in participation rates across the four-year period. Results were broken down into socioeconomic, gender and ethnicity groupings. Additionally, in-depth qualitative research was undertaken, through hour-long, recorded, face-to-face interviews with key players in targeted areas.

The evaluation of the New Deal for Communities (NDC), one of the main area-based regeneration programmes administered by CLG, used a household survey, also by Ipsos MORI, which involved 400 completed questionnaires in all 39 NDC areas plus a benchmark survey of 3,000 people in similarly deprived non-NDC areas. Built on two earlier surveys, and involving many of the same people, this supplied longitudinal data. It also reviewed key area statistics, for example, data on worklessness, education and skills, recorded crime rates (violence, burglary, theft and criminal damage) and health. Further, it included interviews with key players within the NDCs and other agencies and focus groups (Sheffield Hallam University/ Centre for Regional, Economic and Social Research 2006).

Future impact evaluation of new play projects could use a mix of the methods listed above as a template.

Conclusion

The issue of impact evaluation is controversial, as available methodologies are ambiguous and problematic. Quantitative evaluation will be the subject of the second part of this study – Chapter 6 will explore this in greater depth. The next chapter will introduce the qualitative part of this study.

Image: Glamis Adventure Playground

The six case study sites were chosen as examples of good quality, free, staffed play provision and to reflect a diversity of provision types in line with most of today's staffed play provision. Following advice from independent expert Marc Armitage, and in collaboration with the project Advisory Group, the sample includes two successful and acclaimed adventure playgrounds (one of which, Glamis in the London Borough of Tower Hamlets, was voted Best Adventure Playground in London 2007 in a London Play award); two of the most established Play Ranger projects; and two successful play centres. Apart from expert advice on the quality and sustainability of the providers, we chose carefully in order to achieve a geographical mix of projects across the country in a range of rural, suburban and urban settings, as well as some that were in highly ethnically diverse settings, and some in areas that score high on the government's Index of Multiple Deprivation. There follows a brief introduction to the case studies.

Gainsborough Adventure Playground Association

Gainsborough Adventure Playground Association (GAPA) is an independent charity located in Gainsborough (West Lindsey Council, Lincolnshire). It is a free, open-access facility providing a range of indoor and outdoor activities across a two-and-a-half acre site that includes a play centre with various spaces including a facility for under-fives. The centre is located in a post-war, low-density, council housing estate. GAPA has been running for 35 years, although the play centre building has only recently been opened. It is funded by Sure Start, Acis Housing Association, Lincolnshire County Council and West Lindsey District Council, although it also receives other grants, for example from the Big Lottery Fund (BIG), for various projects.

Apart from early years sessions, GAPA is open 3pm–6pm Tuesday to Friday for 5–14-year-olds, who are free to come and go as they please. During the summer holidays, opening hours are longer. In 2007, GAPA recorded 12,976 visits and had approximately 799 children registered as users. This averages out at approximately 419 child visits per month and 299 parent visits per month.

Up to 30 per cent of GAPA's budget was self-generated through voluntary contributions (GAPA recommends a minimum donation of £5 per family per year) and the proceeds from a community café and pass-it-on shop that GAPA runs in a nearby building.

GAPA runs outreach sessions in local parks as well as holding storytelling sessions in the Gainsborough library and participating in annual Playday events.

Glamis Adventure Playground

Glamis Adventure Playground (Glamis) is located in the London Borough of Tower Hamlets. It is a free, open-access facility with an emphasis on outdoor adventure play, on approximately a half-acre site in a densely built-up urban neighbourhood. It also does trips to play sessions in local parks. Glamis reopened in 2002 after eight years of closure; most funding comes from the Big Lottery Fund and money raised as part of Tower Hamlets' Play Matters strategy. Glamis won London Play's Best Adventure Playground of the Year Award for 2007.

The playground is open 3.15pm–8pm Tuesday to Friday and 10am–8pm Saturday; during school holidays and the winter season opening hours differ. On Mondays, Glamis organises a girl's club aimed at reaching out to the large Bengali population in the area. Average daily attendance is approximately 70 children, from a wide range of social, ethnic and ability backgrounds, including around 10 children with special needs. There are four permanent staff members.

Wansdyke Play Association's play ranger project

The Bath and North East Somerset play rangers service started in 2003 and runs free play sessions and activities in parks and open spaces aimed at 5–13-year-olds. The Wansdyke Play Association runs all four projects across the Bath and North East Somerset district, including the site of our case study, Tyning Park in Radstock. This is jointly funded by the Children's Fund and Bath and North East Somerset Council, as well as by various grants, for example, those from the Big Lottery Fund.

In Tyning Park, Radstock, after-school play sessions run twice a week on Mondays and Thursdays from 2.30pm to 5pm, usually with two play rangers present who bring equipment and some snacks to the park, which itself has sparse play equipment and a grassy field with a BMX track. Typical sessions are attended by between 30 and 40 children, with approximately 450 children served by all four sites. There have been recent improvements to the park (planting, a new path and better fencing) after consultation by the play rangers with children and young people.

Children and Young People Participation Service 'Reccy Rangers'

Reccy Rangers, run by the Children and Young People Participation Service (ChYpPS) of Cambridge City Council, provide regular staffed play sessions throughout the year and develop projects in neighbourhoods in response to need. They are also involved in consulting with children and young people about new play and sports facilities.

At our case study site, Abbey Ward, free play sessions are held in different recreation grounds on a weekly basis. Around 270 children and young people aged 9–13 attended Reccy Ranger sessions between April and August 2008, which included the more intensive summer programme. ChYpPS also runs various other projects, such as the 'dec', a bus with computers and games in, which attends one of the recreation grounds twice weekly, BMX sessions and other more structured activities. It is funded using the council's community development budget.

Newbald Church Rooms Young People's Project

The Newbald Church Rooms Young People's Project (East Riding of Yorkshire) opened in 2004. Its aim is to deliver play sessions for children and young people. The project caters for three age groups: 4–9-year-olds, 10–15-year-olds and those aged 15 and over. All groups meet once a week for sessions lasting 90 minutes, 2 hours and 2 hours, respectively, and for longer sessions during school holidays. The club takes place at the centre of the village in a converted church hall and is run by a committee set up as a registered charity; it has no denominational orientation.

Although access is free, parents are charged £5 per month, payable on a voluntary basis, and the project employs three members of staff who are trained playworkers rather than youth workers. Funding was obtained both in kind from the Church of England for the building and from the Big Lottery Fund, as well as from other small donations; by its own estimate, 50 per cent of time put in by staff is voluntary.

Regular attendance per group varies between 20 and 30, with a total of around 200 children in the village. The Church Rooms takes each age group on residential breaks once a year, funded by the Big Lottery Fund. Sessions focus on free play in two indoor rooms and a small, recently refurbished outdoor space; they also include occasional sessions covering issues such as anger management and drug use.

Wythenshawe Community Initiative in Manchester

The Wythenshawe Community Initiative (WCI), based in Manchester, is named after one of the largest low-rise council housing estates in Europe. The service is aimed at children and young people aged between 5 and 11 years and offers open access, free after-school play sessions. It is located in the Woodhouse Park Family Centre, which has three indoor activity rooms and a half-acre outdoor area with differentiated spaces. Due to recent funding cuts the play sessions have been reduced to one per week; average attendance is 40 children per session.

WCI has been funded by Children in Need for the past 11 years and also receives money from the Big Lottery Fund. Some work, such as additional Easter and summer play schemes are funded through Manchester Play and the city council. Wythenshawe is also currently involved in Manchester's 'Parktastic' play ranger scheme.

Image: Reccy Rangers, Cambridge City Council

This chapter provides an in-depth overview and analysis of the key findings of the fieldwork, based on site observations in the six case studies as well as on interviews with children and young people, play provision staff, parents and the wider stakeholders, both policy-makers and front-line delivery staff.

The findings are grouped under seven headings:

1. **Physical setting**, which presents parameters of how the case studies function as physical sites and as 'children's places' within their respective contexts.
2. **Children's stories**, which recounts and analyses the children's responses to these sites and how they relate to them in their daily lives.
3. **Staff stories**, which presents the responses of play provision staff about their professional ethos and objectives, and their ways of working to achieve these.

4. **Making a difference in children's lives**, which presents what children, young people, parents and staff, said about how these play sites impact on the wider lives of young people.

5. **Parents' stories**, which explores parents' perceptions of the play provision sites in terms of how it changes not just their children's lives and their lives as parents, but also the neighbourhood at large, and how this is of value.

6. **Policy partners' responses**, which provides an overview of how a wide range of stakeholders view the role of staffed play provision and how they view discussions about its impact on children's lives and wider benefits.

7. **Institutional links**, which explores how staffed play provision is connected with other aspects of children's services – not just in theory, but also in practice.

1   Physical setting

In a densely built up area, the provision of physical space itself is worth a lot.

(Local area partnership manager, Glamis)

This section presents some key parameters of how the case studies function as physical sites. What emerges is that:

- good quality play provision takes place in a great diversity of physical settings
- there is cross-over between the three main play provision categories studied (play rangers, play centres and adventure playgrounds)
- there is a remarkable contrast between staffed play provision and the wider public realm, and in the way in which these 'children's spaces' provide an extension to and complement the public spaces surrounding them
- each case study is characterised by a diversity of play opportunities within its space
- the six case studies differ in their degree of openness to parents and carers.

Diversity of, and cross-over between, play settings

Staffed play provision takes place across a wide range of physical settings. The six case studies represent this diversity, ranging from a play centre building and garden spanning no more than 50m² to dedicated adventure playgrounds of 2.5 acres. In the case of the play ranger projects in Radstock and Cambridge, a series of parks and dedicated recreation grounds are used as play settings. Equally, WCI and GAPA run regular outreach programmes to extend their provision off site, whilst Glamis and Newbald Church Rooms effectively take on a play ranger role by holding playworker-led sessions in nearby parks and sometimes in schools. Many displayed a cross-over between setting formats. This included one of the adventure playgrounds (GAPA) offering an indoor play centre as well as the more traditional outdoor adventure play. Equally, most providers took children and young people on residentials and trips. Hence, the case studies are characterised by a creative and pragmatic approach by staff to the needs of the area and the possibilities of the sites rather than rigid adherence to one particular provision type.

The wider public realm

What emerged from the research was the often marked contrast between the intensity of use of staffed play settings and the apparent underuse of the surrounding public realm, no matter how potentially amenable to outdoor play it might be. As we shall see in the next sections, this was mirrored by what children and young people said about the public realm. This does not mean the public realm is unimportant, or to be dismissed as a realm for play: on the contrary, it became evident that the routes to play provision sites matter a lot. In Gainsborough and Wythenshawe, children often walked or cycled alone or with friends for significant distances and sometimes were able to draw very elaborate mental maps of their area, indicating the houses of their friends and talking about the route in detail. Conversely, the spatially fragmented and traffic-dominated built environment in Glamis meant that only the most local children could walk; most were brought there by parents or older siblings. This underlines findings in *Seen and Heard* (Beunderman, Hannon and Bradwell 2007) and elsewhere (see for example Lester and Russell 2008) that the good or bad functioning of the public realm as a network of spaces and routes has a great part to play in the spatial freedom of children and in their perception of their everyday world.

All the case study sites are open-access spaces for children, who can come and go as they please, albeit with a brief registration sheet upon entry. The fact that visibility of play settings differ – GAPA and Glamis are very visible as open-air playgrounds whilst the Newbald Church Rooms and WCI are in and behind more traditional buildings – does not seem to make a difference to children's mental maps or ease of access.

What also emerged was that whilst some of the case studies are highly local (Cambridge and Radstock rangers, Newbald and WCI play centres), the two adventure playgrounds draw in children from a much larger area. Whilst most children in GAPA are from the local neighbourhood, it is also frequented by children from across Gainsborough and even by some children from surrounding towns, whose parents bring them there after school or who come with local friends. Equally, whilst most children in Glamis come from the immediate neighbourhood, some are actually driven there from other parts of the borough. In both cases this is seemingly due to the personal network of parents who have heard of these places through word of mouth or because children have local friends or visit local schools; clearly the positive reputation of both places plays an important role here too. In other words, these places are not **just** part of their local public realm – they become destinations for the wider area.

Diversity within the provision

The richness of experiences observed and recounted to us is in large part generated by the fact that each of the four permanent sites, regardless of their size, provide diversity and segmentation within their premises: indoor and outdoor spaces; formal and messy play areas; natural play areas (sandpits, running water, fire pits); fixed equipment spaces for traditional games (football, tag); and hideaways in child-built or pre-provided den spaces. The play ranger projects function through similar, low-interventionist strategies, with children being free to play with or near the rangers or keep their distance and go their own way.

Open spaces, children's spaces

Another key site variable is openness to adults (primarily parents and carers) versus the more deliberate maintenance of a distinct 'children's space'. Policies differ. WCI and Newbald consciously run their sessions as child-only moments; parents are welcome to come in and chat when they drop-off their children or pick them up, but otherwise the space is a parent-free zone. Glamis and GAPA are much more open to the presence of parents on their outdoor premises. This is most marked in Glamis' open-door policy, which leads to many parents spending time there on a sunny day. At those moments, Glamis effectively becomes a local square and functions as a friendly, welcoming (and supervised) extension of the public realm in an area where this is lacking, or difficult to access due to the severance caused by busy roads. Furthermore, both GAPA and WCI function, to a degree, as a community hub, with members of the community able to access parts of the provision just as they access services, or do volunteering work when play sessions are not being run. This permeability of play space is even more the case with the play ranger projects, for obvious reasons, as they deliberately seek to take the institutional offer out into the shared public domain.

That said, even though they might function as 'open institutions' and community hubs, the play sessions are first and foremost run as children's spaces, where both adults and institutions take a secondary role to the needs of children (Moss and Petrie 2002). Each of these sites is different, but all of them are successful because they operate to a site-specific interpretation of the Playwork Principles. This emphasis on free play and children's self-determination marks their contrast to schools, even extended schools, which are an instance of the 'institution opening up to the community' – a welcome concept, but one that does not always mean they go beyond being an institutional space.

2 Children's stories

You can really play here. They have a football here, and other things, there's nice food ... every day I go here until it closes.

(Boy, 8, GAPA)

This section recounts and analyses the children's responses about the case study sites and how they relate to them in their daily lives. What emerges is that:

- staffed play provision gives children more to do and intensifies opportunities to play compared to other places
- childrens experiences show a marked difference between the case studies and public parks
- staff members make an important contribution to children and young people's experience
- socialising with others, including older and younger children, is a crucial part of what children do when at the case study sites;
- trusted, personal relations with staff members are highly valued by children and young people
- children are often actively involved in changing physical elements of the play setting
- there is a mixed picture about where children would be if they did not attend the play provision in our case studies.

The quote above is not from an unhappy child with nowhere to go. When asked about his neighbourhood, he says he goes 'pretty much everywhere': he cycles around on his bike, goes to the local park with its fixed equipment playground, and sometimes goes with his grandma to the river which passes through the town. But still, he says, GAPA is an important place because 'these other places are more, like, boring – here you can **play**', he emphasises.

More to do

This boy's answer to our questions is typical of what children and young people say about their neighbourhoods, and about how staffed play provision fits into it. Consider what a 13-year-old girl says about her area, the park in Radstock where the Bath and North East Somerset play rangers go:

The area's all right, but a bit boring. There's nothing much to do around; I go here or to Radstock park, they are the only two places. This park is funner with the rangers; they bring more people, more things to play with. I only really go here every Monday or Thursday when the rangers are here – not really otherwise. We play, cook things, play tag; I love taking care of K— [the 2-year-old toddler son of a neighbour], I meet friends here, we do lots of different stuff really. That's why it's different from other parks. It's so much more fun.

We hear the same stories again and again across our case studies: staffed play provision, whether through rangers in the public parks or in play centres and adventure playgrounds, intensifies opportunities to play and have fun. This points to a clear role for staff, as specified in the Playwork Principles, to facilitate play. The role of staff lies in the removal of, or to aid in negotiating, barriers to this process – whether contextual, physical or attitudinal.

The difference with parks

Those children and young people interviewed almost invariably held strongly positive opinions about play provision, emphasising how they could play freely, meet their mates and how they saw opportunities for engaging in all sorts of activity because of the play provision, the staff and what they bring. The contrast with the general public realm was remarkable: parks are mostly described as boring, with nothing to do, or as a place where they are not allowed to go. In some cases, the situation was even more poignant: as in an 8-year-old boy's story of a park where Cambridge's ChYpPS Reccy Rangers go:

I think the park is horrible and unsafe, people take drugs and vandalise things … but I like it when the ChYpPS come 'cause I have fun with them … I only really like it when they are here, they make it safe, I learned to have fun 'cause I never had fun before, and I don't really go out on the street other days.

Play provision, in other words, brings possibility. The variety of play experiences observed in the fieldwork and mentioned in the interviews is endless, from football to building dens, from 'making stuff' (art, bow and arrows, gloop to throw around) to water fights, from climbing trees and inventing games with swings and jumping from ever higher platforms to making fire, and from role play and dress-up to cooking a wide range of food. Having these opportunities brought into the public realm positively animates spaces that children otherwise view as dangerous, forbidding or simply dull. How children value this is also evident in how much time most of them seem to spend there: a clear majority in all case studies respond that they 'come when it opens and stay until it closes' or until the play rangers leave. It seems as if they will not miss a minute.

What staff can bring

The role of the staff is crucial – although often in an indirect way, as an 11-year-old boy from Glamis makes clear: 'They say hello and make you sign in but then let you get on with it.' This is in contrast to what children experience elsewhere. A girl in Newbald explains:

> at Brownies we are told what to do, but here you go and you are free, only when you are being too silly they might tell you to stop.

And a group of boys in Manchester comment:

> The grown-ups are great … they leave you alone but if you can't do something they do it with you, like making stuff or face painting; they play along with basketball and football, and think of new games … plus it's important that they are there in case you hurt yourself.

In other words, what the children describe is a balance between freedom and intervention, between being able to do what they want and knowing that it's okay even if something happens. Relationships predicated on the values of play also extend beyond the site, as multiple children and young people, when asked about a recent favourite activity, mentioned the trips and residentials they have been on. Being away with mates and playworkers as opposed to being away with school or with parents, or not going away at all (the reality for many of the children in these neighbourhoods), is an important experience. What counts, in the perception of the youngsters, is the social possibility – whether within the confines of the site or elsewhere:

> We come here to meet friends; they don't come out so often in Radstock. Here you can just go and you know they are there. There

is less fighting, people feel relaxed and safe, everyone plays with each other and that's great.

(Girl, 14, Radstock)

Socialising with others

A particularly important role fulfilled by some of the settings is the bringing together of children and young people who may live in the same area but go to different schools and who would therefore not otherwise be in contact. This is the case in Newbald, where many children go to different state or private schools and would live separate lives were it not for the 'village hub'. The difference between the 'children's place' and the 'institutional place' becomes even more marked, with the children's place a more natural part of the geographical locality than the more segmented institutional world.

The importance of such contact is not just between same-age peers; contact with children of different ages is mentioned frequently and is evident from our observations, from the girl in Radstock, who spends most of her time in the park with 2-year-old K— and his mum, to the 10-year-old girl in Newbald, who says that in the Church Rooms 'the teenagers are very friendly, and then also in the park we all know each other, you know they might be drunk or so but they are still really nice to us'. In other words, in these settings they have contact with others in ways that they do not elsewhere. It seems that as a result of this, many young people become quite caring of younger children and also feel cared for. In Gainsborough, an 11-year-old says:

> *It's like a youth club here really, but for 0–14s … It's nice having the ages, because of course at my age it's important that you mix with little kids as well as big kids. It's nice because the little kids will play with you and stuff, but the big kids, they'll do more dangerous stuff with you.*

This is a key contrast with unstaffed playgrounds, which are often dominated by certain age groups that all too often exclude others. Conversely, the atmosphere in staffed settings is one of togetherness and cooperation rather than age standoff and territorialism. Through operating as a resource and refuge, staff members offer a moderated social experience where cross-age socialisation between children allows opportunities to build and maintain diverse social networks and to develop a children's culture in the knowledge that adults are there should the children require them. Research by Harlow and Suomi (1971) suggests that cross-age socialisation is more effective than same-age socialisation in overcoming the effects of deprivation as it provides opportunities to practise caring and being cared for play.

A very personal relationship

One specific element that needs to be mentioned is the close relation between some children and staff members. Many children and young people clearly value that relation, as is evident both in what they say and how they behave around staff, loudly greeting the Bath and North East Somerset play rangers when they arrive in Radstock's Tyning Park. For older teenagers, who still sometimes visit the park when the rangers are present, this is a cherished memory of earlier years:

Yeah we came down here every day. We used to sit on our own table and drink hot chocolate together … like, I talked to her about my mum and me arguing all the time, cause me and my mum don't get along so I used to talk with C— about it. She don't mind us like talking to her.

(Girl, 16)

In Newbald, one girl (8) tells the same story: 'You can trust them with something, like say you've got a secret, you can just tell them'. As such, the staff play an important go-between role – one which makes a difference in the lives of young people. Like Radstock, some of the teenagers in Newbald continue frequenting the Church Rooms service despite having outgrown it. Their reflections add to the story. As one 15-year-old boy says:

They're the ones who always stick up for us when people around the village say 'all the kids around here'; they seem to think we're all terrible. We've all got a bad reputation for no reason, but [the playworkers] are the ones who always stick up for us in the pub and that.

The relationship clearly continues over time, as for another boy (18):

They're there for you, in a sense. If you don't want to talk to your mum and dad you can always come and talk to them. I don't think there's that many teenagers that get that.

In many cases this is particularly important as children may be in vulnerable circumstances, which playworkers confirm is often the case. The fact that teenagers keep turning back to the trusted, one-to-one relationships they have built is clear evidence of the important and ongoing roles these playworkers have in their lives. In these stories, a 'play philosophy' which values individual choice, expression and development in a supportive, rather than judgemental, setting visibly characterises relationships between playworkers and children – relationships which cross boundaries of age, time and the site itself.

Making it yourself – and giving back

In many cases children and young people have been involved, to some degree, in the design and building or maintenance of the play sites. This can be a source of considerable pride, and is mentioned by some young people as the favourite thing they ever did. As one girl in Radstock says, they created a BMX track, planted new greenery and put in benches, getting funding for it 'by telling D— what to write and he wrote a letter and then my sister and brother went to a conference in London to win it'. In Glamis, too, the appreciation of these constructive contributions is evident, as one girl (8) says:

Everything's made out of wood. I quite like it you know, because children have helped make all these things. You see those swings and those paintings? All the children have done that. All the painting and everything. Everybody chooses the colour. They want to listen to us, they want to know what's nice, and so we get what we wanted.

Equally, a boy from Newbald reflects that: 'I've been helping on the weekend; I've been digging and that. It's been good just to put something into it after I've got so much out of it.'

These quotes articulate the cycle of change in both the site and the children who attend it. As children 'age-through', rather than 'age-out', the nature of their involvement and contribution changes according to individual ability and inclination. By offering opportunities for individual and collective decision-making, whereby children can see the concrete environmental consequences of their decisions, play providers create ways for children to engage and become stakeholders, and to continually refashion their play environment to suit their own changing needs.

Where else would they be?

Crucial in this discussion is a question regarding the additional opportunities offered by these staffed projects: 'If they weren't here or could not come here anymore, where would they be or go?' In today's climate of fear for and of children and young people, the story appears twofold: on the one hand there is a category of children and young people who would be outside anyway, but would have a less positive experience or 'get in trouble'; on the other hand, many children would find themselves at home more, without friends. Neither case appeared attractive to them.

Characteristic of the first category is what one girl (13) says in Radstock:

> It keeps us out of trouble, otherwise we'd be on the road and that would be dangerous with the traffic. The park is usually empty when they are not here … if the rangers weren't here we would not go out so much; we'd just go to Radstock park and hang out there, but there isn't much to do.

The second issue is well put by a girl (8) from Glamis:

> It's especially nice because I want to have fun. The computer's boring, even though we have internet. I'm going to become a naughty girl if I keep going on the computer and if I'm not going to get any fresh air.

For both of these groups, staffed but open-access play provision serves as a middle ground where they can be both safe and free. Their use of this freedom – to engage in social interaction and enjoy themselves – often leads to a deep affection for the place that marks it out as 'special' among other public spaces.

An 11-year-old boy in Newbald says:

> I love it here. I always help tidying up at the end of the day. Without this I would mess about and make trouble, here I can **play**.

In Gainsborough, two girls (9 and 10) are equally clear, commenting, one after the other, that:

> If not here, you'd be stuck at home and be bored all the time…

> I'm not allowed to go to St George playground, mum does not take me there and I'm not allowed to go there alone but here I can come on my own.

Also evident is a real division between children, between those who have many places to go to and those who don't. But even those who have options, such as the boy quoted at the beginning of this section, still value what's on offer within the case study sites. An indication of this is when they tell stories about things 'you only do here'. A boy (9) in Glamis says:

> Here you make new things, you can really play and do what you want, like I learned how to be [an] actor in a talent show.

Different children have different needs from the same provision, so for some the site is most important as a 'place to go to' and be with friends, whilst for others it is what that site offers – art supplies, an environment safe for experimental play, sympathetic adults – that is important. An emphasis on the particular needs of each child ensures that they are all accessing a site conducive to individual self-determination.

Animation of the public realm

What emerges from these stories is the sense of animation and activity that emanates from good quality play provision, no matter what type. Children see this as an intensification of opportunity for different types of behaviour, diverse play and socialisation. It strongly follows that it is the staff who turn these places into real areas of opportunity, and that it is this enriching experience that makes these places stand out for children. Regardless of whether – and this differs enormously for each case study and indeed for each child – children feel safe and confident to go and be in the public realm generally, these sites of play provision are sites of special intensity; they are special destinations on children's mental maps.

Reflecting on these findings, there are clear indications of the types of value that emerge and of how they connect with wider trends and discussions. There has been recognition that even the last decade's increased investment in the public realm has not been sufficient to create an animated public sphere (see Beunderman and Lownsbrough; also see for more information initiatives such as Streets Alive, the CLG-funded Street Games programme, and the CABE publication *Parks Need Parkforce* 2005). The value of intergenerational contact outside the immediate peer group has seen increasing interest (Margo and others 2006).

Finally, there has been an increased emphasis on personal relations as an underpinning principle for any public service (see Craig and Skidmore 2005, Heapy and Parker 2005, Bartlett and Leadbeater 2008). What children said to us is that such principles are being put into practice in these places. The very special meaning that this has for them is perhaps best summed up by one girl (9) who says about GAPA that 'it's a nice happy house-like place, not home but still a nice place to come'.

3   Staff stories

This section presents the responses of play provision staff to questions about their professional ethos and objectives and their ways of working to achieve these. What emerges is that:

- playwork staff invariably have a strong ethic and they see their key role as 'setting a setting' for play, as facilitating rather than directing what children do
- this implies the use of directed intervention as a 'safety net' and the offering of reflections on problematic situations
- outreach to under-represented groups is increasingly integral to daily practice in these case studies
- playworkers see themselves as connected to the wider context of the locality and they work beyond the boundaries of the provision site to generate wider play opportunities.

A playworker at WCI talks about a session they run as part of Manchester City Council's Parktastic scheme, a three-year funded play ranger programme across the city delivered by third sector play organisations.

> *We had a brilliant session one Monday where we went into the park and just went in with minimal stuff, we took a metal detector, a football and four juggling balls and just literally that's all we took. And they're used to us normally carrying a sack with us, so there were a few questions, you know 'why you not bringing more equipment'. So we explained we've come here with our imaginations … And we took a step back and we realised we had done the perfect job that day at the session because the children were just getting on with it with everything we got, even with minimal equipment, it was brilliant to see, we were facilitating rather than getting involved.*
>
> (Playworker, WCI)

The story demonstrates how play is not about the equipment, or even necessarily the site. Instead, it is the team of playworkers and the children who create a social space, collectively constructing a place for play. It is this emphasis on facilitation rather than guidance, on imagination rather than materials, which distinguishes good playwork.

Setting a setting

What the WCI playworker talks about is at the core of what most staff members mention as their key role, namely, to intervene minimally in order to generate the greatest benefit for children. The intensification of play opportunity that emerged in the children's stories as a key defining characteristic of staffed provision seems rooted in this strong commitment to free play rather than to guided activities; risk-taking, inventiveness, the use of imagination and learning from peers emerge as some of the most precious elements of playwork. This does not mean that staff do not intervene. On the contrary, in many cases it was emphasised that the success of these places depends strongly on the setting of ground rules to enable the full and complex diversity of play to take place. As a playworker in Glamis emphasises, in an area where gang violence and territorialism are real issues, there is a need to manage play provision:

> *so that the children feel more comfortable; create a space and atmosphere and environment where kids can do as they please. Tolerance is key, creating a place where a boy can dress up, even dress up like a girl if he pleases, without being laughed at … so our role is to provide some interventions to sustain that atmosphere.*

In this the playworker's role is one of facilitation – what they facilitate is the collective maintenance of the site as one of tolerance, openness, support and possibility.

Part of this role is in the expanding of children's horizons: offering new opportunities for play, new experiences that children would otherwise not have. From cooking on an open fire and carving with knives to face painting and taking children on walks through the neighbourhood, all these are ways of increasing the number of experiences, both by offering new ideas and by responding to children's ideas. Amongst all the different practices of a site, it is this role that seems to make all the difference for children when they comment that many conventional, fixed and unstaffed playgrounds are 'boring'. As the same Glamis playworker puts it:

> *Using tools and experiencing the elements is a core part of play … ideally they'd have the confidence and skills to get on with those things themselves but city life isn't like that and there's this risk obsession … what we aim to give is experiences that they would not have otherwise in their childhood, allowing them to be creative, able to experiment, test confidence without adults directing them, socialise, and build up relationships.*

Staffed play provision can be seen as creating a compensatory environment for children, one that is fit for their needs where the wider environment is not. One part of this is offering support and assistance to children in developing their independence.

Offering reflections

Another role is to reflect with children and young people on the limits of behaviour and about risks constituted both through external dangers and in social situations. A particularly powerful story is told by the director of the Newbald Church Rooms:

We had three 13-year-olds. One had the potential of being bullied, and the other two were very very strong and potential bullies. They were trying to see how much pain they could instil in the others, by putting them on their backs with one leg crossed over the other and pushing back. It was horrible to watch, really horrible. We had the conversation 'are you all okay with this' and they said they were. We said 'have you thought about broken bones' and they said they had. And we said 'are you going to continue' and they said yes. I decided to let them continue, but I stayed in the room. I felt a bit sick to watch, to be honest, and they did continue, but as I say I hated it. I mentioned it to the potential victim afterwards, because he's a sensible lad, so I said 'what was that all about?' He said 'I have to prove myself to be okay, I have to prove that I'm strong, but I wouldn't have dared do that anywhere else. But because you were there I felt safe. Thank you.' Because he knew that if anything happened I could have stepped in. What he was saying basically was that because I was there he could do something that he had to do, or else he would have done it at another time when it would have been less safe. That's why we have to be so careful not to intervene.

This example shows how playworkers often position themselves as a resource or refuge on site, meaning that they are there if the children need them. In this role, they sometimes find themselves in difficult situations like the one described above. However, it is clear from the boy's response that for him, the staff's position as a 'safety net' helped him 'play through' something he felt was important in a safer and more moderated way than would have otherwise been possible. Central to the role of the staff is the concept of reflective practice and the sharing of stories, such as this one, between themselves to continually evaluate provision and provide support within the team.

These multiple learning experiences are what children value. This becomes clear through the story of a playworker, who used to come to GAPA when young and whose deep personal commitment is intricately linked to what she experienced then:

I grew up here. I learned to write my name here, I learned to roller-skate. I learned everything fun here. It was the sense of adventure, anything's possible. You can make anything you want out of anything you want, and it's right. If you make it, it's right, because it's what you see. That's what I learned here, how to make mistakes and accept them ... They don't get to play like that anymore; they don't get to do mischievous things anymore. They're just labelled. It's cruel to them. We used to go on bike rides when I was a kid for miles, but you can't today. So something like this gives them some freedom. They're free to express themselves. Yeah, they fall over, they hurt themselves, but they can play.

The chance to make mistakes, to use the 'safety net' of adults as a fall-back option whilst exploring one's own capacities and that of the site, is at the heart of free play.

Reaching out

Whilst such quotes hardly do justice to the complexities of playwork, they do hold up a mirror to what children experience. The playwork ethic, as it could be called, forms a deliberately flexible, enabling infrastructure. In the words of one WCI staff member:

I think what makes us different is that we try not to speak to them like they're in a school service, we try and have an understanding of each child, reaching a level with each of them and making it work for them instead of monitoring them.

One particular aspect of this is that staff, in most cases, were very aware of the need to reach a wider audience through outreach programmes in order to increase their appeal to groups currently under-represented in using the provision. In some cases, such as Glamis and WCI, there were staff resources allocated specifically to this; for example, for reaching out to established and new ethnic minority communities or disabled children. One particular example is the drive, in Glamis, to increase take-up by the local Asian population. This led, for example, to an effort to improve the physical condition of the site and green it in order to give it a better first impression for those parents less familiar with the concept of the adventure playground.

Slightly closer behaviour management was also part of this agenda, as was personalised effort to show the site to parents and explain how it was managed and the activities available. As a playworker in the centre says:

Bengali parents and kids are perhaps rather cautious, they need to see it's okay and hear it through word of mouth from other parents.

Similarly, Glamis appointed staff to work with learning disabled children, leading to an increase in numbers attending which, whilst it may seem relatively small (up to five new learning disabled children in the last season), potentially has a large impact on the lives of the children and young people involved:

> We see that there is more and more mixing between the assisted kids and the others depending on there being more children on the playground, if the site and the types of play it allows are more diverse, if there is more going on then they can better fit in, wherever they want; other kids will help, interact, do different things. And seeing lots of kids do things will motivate these children with behaviour issues to engage and do things themselves.

The increase in the use of the service indicated here is remarkable: Glamis' own figures show that the average attendance per day overall has gone up, in the last three years, from 10 to 30 in winter, and in summer from 35 to 70.

In sum, when they are successful, these places provide opportunities for cross-cultural engagements, for children to play together who otherwise would not, and in so doing to learn, share and practice a range of skills with long-term social, physical and developmental benefits – not to mention the immediate increase in the children's quality of daily life.

Beyond the boundaries

One last point to mention explicitly is that all staff showed strong idealism beyond the confines of the actual play setting. They did not see their workplace as disconnected from the locality, but rather as part of the fabric of the neighbourhood, either physically or organisationally, and conceived of themselves as part of the localised infrastructure for children and young people. Whilst we will pick up on this later, it is evident in working practices: for the play rangers, such engagement with the wider public realm is their very *raison d'être*. It also shows in the ways in which, for example, Glamis staff take children for neighbourhood walks; Manchester WCI is a delivery partner for the local Parktastic scheme, GAPA delivers play days and outreach sessions across Gainsborough; and the Newbald Church Rooms uses the local park on a monthly basis, and provides an open house for teenagers who fall outside the main focus group for the project but still regularly come back. This commitment is perhaps best phrased by one Manchester playworker who says that:

there has been quite a lot of stigma attached to parks in the last few years, so they just need a small reminder that the parks are there for them to enjoy, they can climb trees and make themselves dens with natural resources, it's fun, adventurous ... and I hope we are getting somewhere with that.

Intervention in a style appropriate to the setting is one of the key challenges and skills of playwork. As Paul Bonel and Jennie Lindon have suggested:

There is a distinction to be made between play and playwork. Play is something that children engage in of their own free will. It is in no way essential for adults to be part of children's play and, often, children's play goes on to the total exclusion of adults. However, for play to take place in a free and spontaneous way the conditions have to be right.

(1996: 14)

This may involve acknowledging the importance of risky and apparently not very 'positive' behaviour, but all these aspects of play must be seen as interconnected and mutually dependent (Lester and Russell 2008). This third section has outlined some stories of how staff are keenly aware of this as underpinning the creation of children's places.

4 Making a difference in children's lives

I am going to another school because I have problems, ADHD. I've got friends here. It's good, means I have people to play with. My Mum don't let me out much. I only come here when my sister [a playworker] is here. I've learned how to make stuff. I'm an arty person, I hadn't thought to make art stuff before, but now I do ... and I like climbing trees, only here I can do that ... I'm better at school because of here ... even if some people wind me up at school ... I just ignore them.

(Boy, 9, GAPA)

This section presents what children, young people, parents and staff said about how these play sites impact on the wider lives of young people. What emerges is that:

● children mention many elements of 'learning' as a natural aspect of the play experience and how this is about learning to learn as much as about learning actual things

- children talk about their experiences in terms of trajectories of progress how they are overcoming initial difficulties, both social and physical
- there are many life skills and attitudes towards others that children say they obtain as part of this process
- for children, such experiences can be connected to a wider outlook on life
- parents and others who are involved confirm indications that play provision contributes to a growth in children's 'capabilities'.

A crucial question is whether, as children and young people enjoy and appreciate the different play provision sites investigated, their lives change for the better. Children's lives are inevitably shaped by a large range of factors, which can either be positive contributors to their quality of life and well-being or profoundly and appallingly negative. Children's lives are complex and often difficult, but what they tell us is important – and they tell us that these places are important to them. Access to free play opportunities can be extraordinarily beneficial for children in many ways, and it is worth remembering that this provision may make a difference in ways we do not understand and cannot quantify.

Generally speaking, the six case studies took place in the context of various degrees of social deprivation. Many of the projects and programmes visited were located in neighbourhoods that score high in the government's statistics on social exclusion and deprivation, although that does not mean they were visited exclusively by local children who would fit that statistical profile. A complex social context is, however, inevitably the background against which stories about the impact of play should be seen. In this section we will focus on what children and young people themselves said about this. What they spoke about was a continuum between, first, the concrete skills or abilities they had gained, second, life skills or attitudes that had changed and third, their sense of well-being and outlook on life more generally, even in sometimes stressful circumstances.

Elements of 'learning'

Children and young people often used the word 'learning' without being specifically prompted. When asked about the things they liked doing, they would often mention things they had learned to do. In many cases, they were quite happy to be more specific when asked. They spoke about it in different ways. Consider what a 9-year-old girl from Glamis says:

We invent new games, like making obstacles with wood and then that's a challenge and you have 20 seconds to do it … and pirate games. Or you can make up games with the swings and building blocks. I learned to light fires, cook, what plants are edible … stuff that was petrifying isn't here … I come here because it's great and I get to do really fun stuff.

In this story, elements of learning are part of a general set of activities that have to do with inventing games and overcoming challenges. In other words, the learning does not seem formalised as such, instead becoming a natural part of what goes on in the playground. Consider what a 14-year-old girl from Radstock says:

Before the rangers came I never really went anywhere – there weren't really any places to go, but they're great they've taught me to build tents, do barbeques safely, lots of little things I couldn't do before.

Lots of little things – that seems to be the key. When asked to be more explicit, the children seemed to get a little impatient, as in fact these 'little things' were self-evident to them. However, they are happy to reflect; take this 10-year-old boy from GAPA:

It feels safe [here] and you get to learn how to be safe. You get to learn how to do things and you can do those things somewhere else too. When we made a den it was really hard and we managed to work it out. We managed to.

In these play settings, children did not just learn how to 'do things', they learnt how to learn – whilst enjoying themselves. They explored and expanded their own capacity for enjoyment, boldness and curiosity. They had a range of experiences and emotions, primary as well as secondary.

Making friends and feeling supported by them as well as by the workers is often intrinsic to this process:

I learned to play football and roller-skating and learned how to make friends. If I feel bad, people make you feel better … you make friends and they make you feel better.

(Boy, 8, GAPA)

It's because you're around everyone as well. Say you're stuck on something you're making and you thought you could make it but you couldn't really. If you just ask them they'll help you paint and everything. That's what I like.

(Girl, 9, Glamis)

There are also hints that the play sites are different, in all this, to formal settings. As a girl from Newbald says:

at school boys and girls can't be friends, it's not that we're not allowed but if we're friends then everyone thinks we're boyfriend and girlfriend … and we're too young to be like that. That doesn't happen here. It's okay to play with boys here.

Trajectories of progress

For many children, play provision offers opportunities to explore, practise and share a range of skills – including social ones. Progression and the mastery of difficulty are evident in what this boy (9) from Glamis says:

I met these [boys] when I came, I didn't want to talk to them because I didn't know them a lot, but when we came here I thought I might as well play with them, didn't know anyone else to play with. So I went up to them and I said 'let's play a game'. Then we played a game and we really got to know each other a lot. Being together is fun and it helps you to learn more.

There are endless versions of this story, as children describe the shyness of the first day, the wait until someone runs up to them and says hello, or the girl from GAPA who was afraid to explore the full extent of the grounds but now likes den-building in 'top corner' as it's no longer 'scary'. They speak of a growing facility with the place and its inhabitants, and of social and physical skills. This is brilliantly captured by one girl from Glamis:

You know, some people feel scared and stuff but you come here and you know the funny things around here, right, a) it teaches you stuff not to be afraid of, b) it makes you forget about all your worries. I was proper freaked out when I came in here and I looked at that swing, but when I started coming I started forgetting about my fear and I started doing it from a high point. They were all like 'whoa, she's just getting here for like three weeks and she's standing on the high point'. I don't mind, I'm brave.

Here she demonstrates how improving play skills can confer added benefits, such as self-confidence, a sense of achievement and agency. The important point here is not that children are acquiring or practising skills for long-term practical benefit, but to improve their lives here and now, to enable them to become better players today.

Life skills and attitudes

What is crucial to note is that these effects arise out of children's experiences, not because of formal learning situations. It is the increased interaction with their peers that seems to make all the difference to children such as this boy (9, GAPA):

> *It's like, a lesson [being here]. One big lesson where you can learn different things in one lesson. It's really good. Being brave, making stuff. Pogo sticks and that dragon. We have lots of adventures.*

This includes overcoming feelings of negativism or sadness, which inevitably occur in the lives of children, through providing time and space for a different kind of experience. Asked to describe what would happen when she visited GAPA on a hypothetical day that 'wasn't nice because of something happening at school or at home', one girl (8) answers: 'You can have some peace and quiet and step out of it and forget ... I'd feel better because of the other people here'. This mirrors what a boy (11) from Newbald says: 'When I feel down my friends here make me laugh and cheer me up.'

At other times, the difference lies in the individual child's approach to problems. For example, the same boy goes on to explain other ways in which he's changing:

> *You have fun, you do what you want but you also share and look after each other ... when I was younger I did not share stuff so I learned that and how to help when someone is hurt.*

Stories like this are many – children are lucid about their shortcomings and how they change through interaction. One girl says:

> *Some people come here and then they are rude to you, but I come here so I can stop their being rude to other people. I can make them understand what they do to other people, and help. That's why I come here.*

Or take this girl from GAPA, who says:

> *I also learned a lesson about being kind, at first I was mucking about and saying nasty things and some of the staff and the children taught me that wasn't nice and now I get along better with the others.*

Many children have been both bullied and bullies themselves at different times. As such, learning social skills of kindness, sharing and resilience in the face of adversity are not just valuable but are essential for happiness. The playground offers many the chance to 'start again' within a new social environment, and to learn how to do things differently. In Glamis, one girl (10) talks about the difference between where she lives and the adventure playground:

It's too quiet and the kids around me bully me a lot because I've got a small finger. I've got only one friend where I live, but I have loads of friends here.... Being around other children has made me less shy and come out of my shell and stuff to say hello. When I didn't come here I used to be really quiet and I didn't talk to anybody but now that I've come here I know everybody, talk to everybody.

Stories like this abound, reminding us of the many factors that shape young people's lives. For example, this girl (9, Glamis) describes:

I think it's helped me at school because I used to get bullied at school but now I don't because [my friend] said to me whenever you're sad, think of the Adventure Park because it's really bright and happy.

In other words, whilst we should be under no illusion about knowing the full extent of children's lives and the difficulties they might face, from their own stories it emerges that they are capable of pointing to particular sociable experiences, linked to the play setting, that changes who they are and how they feel.

An outlook on life

In some instances the positive stories from the play setting seem to circulate much more widely and be part of a more positive outlook than children might have of their everyday world. Statements such as 'When I am here I feel really happy' (girl, 9, WCI) and 'I feel loads better because I'm not so lonely and everyone makes mates. It's really nice' (girl, 10, Cambridge) show unambiguously how the children associate the sites with having a good time. A boy (9) from Glamis puts it this way:

If kids don't [have adventures] they won't learn anything ... well they will, because they'll go to school, but they just won't learn to have fun if they don't have adventures and do stuff. They'll just do the same things, like school. I think adventures are good for you, you learn stuff in the adventure.

In this conversation, when asked what happens when children don't have adventures, he expands: 'They get bored, they get told off in school because they're bored and they don't pay attention. Lots of stuff. That used to be me, but not anymore.' It becomes clear that, whilst the play space is for some a 'break' from the rest of their lives, it can also function as a way of providing critical distance and different experiences that can then inform the child's strategy of living outside the site itself.

Another powerful account comes from a girl in Newbald, who links how she feels about the Church Rooms and the village:

This place makes me think the village is nice, the best place to live and share. I think the village is really peaceful, it's a really nice place to live in. You know like in Hull, there's loads of kidnappers and stuff, but here this is a really calm village. You see people walking and you can say hello and they'll say hello back. People are nice to this place [the Church Rooms] also, they give in shoeboxes and craft stuff if they don't use it so that we can play with it. Even the teenagers can be alright. If you're upset they can come up and say 'what's up with you then' and make you laugh.

She goes on to say that she would like to work with children later, as she likes 'helping them'.

The role of teenagers who might have otherwise 'aged-out' of the sites is evident from the stories they tell. Attendance at such sites has frequently contributed to shaping their thoughts and aspirations, as in the case of one boy (18) who is now on the management committee of Newbald Church Rooms:

M— wanted a younger perspective [on the committee] and I've always been involved in quite a lot of stuff. On trips and that I've always helped out. You can put it on your CV can't you, and say 'I've done this'. It's like being Head Boy and that isn't it? It's volunteer work, so employers think 'oh, he must be quite good because he's done this and that'. It makes you feel good, don't it? It makes you more confident because you have to hang out with people you don't really know.

Children and young people have different needs from the site, and it is always a delicate balance to ensure that one group is not pushed out by another. However, some of these case studies demonstrate that the needs of the two groups are not necessarily mutually exclusive and that they might benefit tremendously from being and playing together.

Reflecting on stories of change

Children and young people tell us endless stories of change and personal growth, in anything from practical abilities through to crucial life skills in difficult circumstances and boldness in facing new challenges. They themselves clearly link these things, at least partially, to the play settings they enjoy, and it goes some way to explaining parents' remarks such as 'You can always tell when it's Monday or Thursday, they can't wait for the days that the rangers are here, they always ask about them' (Mother of three children, Radstock).

Parents' stories of how this change in their child happens can equally range from the practical and everyday – the same Radstock mother says 'They are quieter when the rangers have been, they get proper tired, it stops them from raiding the cupboards and the fridge or munch crisps, it gets them active' – to the profound, as evident from this mother of an autistic son in GAPA: 'My autistic son learns social interaction here and artistic skills, they can interact on their own terms which he can't in the classrooms, here there's a choice for them to be alone or mix.'

Similarly, the staff interviewed tell varying tales about how individual children have changed. A few examples come from the WCI playworker cited earlier in this section:

One or two children I've noticed that their anger has reduced and they are a lot more social with the children and they're not bullying the other children. And they are reacting a lot more to one another than they used to. I think the two children you met earlier are classic examples, I don't know if they are just growing up or we are having an impact on them. But they used to argue with one another quite a lot and sometimes with the other children, but the other few weeks when I've been observing them, I've noticed they're not fighting with one another as much and getting into as many ruckuses.

Such might be the stories of change over a short time – but equally this might apply to change over a longer time period. One GAPA staff member describes how a boy with learning difficulties has become involved in the running of the playground:

We've got one kid, he's got his own set of personal problems. He turned 15 and was too old to come so we got him back as a young volunteer. There was nothing else for him. He doesn't go to school. We wanted him to have something to do, something useful.

These are stories about individuals and how they change in ways that, in the words of the local vicar and chair of Glamis, 'are long-term, invisible to the eye, and non-quantifiable, but they are there'. However, even the most seemingly elusive of play benefits can have clear and noticeable effects, as one detached youth worker based in the area around Glamis confirms unambiguously:

The area is different because of Glamis – particularly mixing between the different ethnic groups did not happen so much before [it re-opened], now we have real interaction here instead of the ethnic bubbles in which different groups lived, and it happens earlier in age as well – which is important because barriers are really broken down when they are younger, you get conditioned and realise it is better to live together … they have shared experiences at that place that they take out to the world.

In Newbald, the chair of the parish council speaks from experience when he says that 'the youngsters learn crucial things like negotiation, turn-taking in those situations beyond school, in real life outside institutions … the education system is too much about instruction instead of experiences'. As chair, he sees the difference in how the young approach him:

The Church Rooms keep the lines of communication open between children and young people and [the] rest of town; the ones who go there talk to me confidently … others not so much. Even though it's difficult to say which is cause and which effect, there is a difference between attenders and non-attenders. For example at our AGM, when a developer's proposal to build on the play park was discussed, it was the children from the Church Rooms (or those who had been there in the past) who came to put in a very balanced argument about the playground. They were 15 or 16 years old or so, but very lucid and articulated and calm, and clear, more so than some of the adults … I put a lot of that down to the good work that the Church Rooms are doing.

We will return to the experiences of policy-makers and other stakeholders later, but these anecdotes paint a compelling picture of how good quality play provision has an impact on children and, in turn, on the locality in which they live. Crucially, what we see here is how children and young people indirectly talk about the learning of what Amartya Sen and Martha Nussbaum call 'capabilities': positive freedoms that are at the core of a person's ability to be or do something (as opposed to 'negative' freedoms which focus on the absence of interferences) (Sen 1979, Nussbaum and Sen 1993). On Nussbaum's list of core capabilities crucial to any democracy (Nussbaum 2000) are elements such as:

- being able to use the senses, to imagine, think and reason
- being able to use imagination and thought in connection with experiencing and producing works and events of one's own choice
- human association that can be shown to be crucial in the development of emotions, emotional attachments and affiliations
- being able to form a conception of the good and to engage in critical reflection about the planning of one's life
- being able to laugh and to enjoy recreational activities.

These 'capabilities' are vitally important both for children's quality of life today and for the future. We will discuss these issues in greater detail in the next chapter, but in a country that was ranked at the bottom of the league table for children's well-being in developed economies (UNICEF 2007), and where concepts of a 'good childhood' are the subject of soul-searching and debate (see the Good Childhood enquiry which can be viewed via the Children's Society website, accessed 10 October 2008), the stories told by the children we interviewed send a powerful message as to possible sources of positive contribution to their happiness and development.

5   Parents' stories

My kids come here every week ... they would not miss it. You drop them every now and then and think that's good ... there aren't other places for them you know, not without travelling or without me, they'd always go to the park with us, I would not ever let them out on the street alone.... It's the freedom but it's also a safety-conscious place, with good quality equipment ... when they come away they are really full of it, full of enthusiasm, after doing some cooking class she made me a pancake at home ... it gives me a couple of hours off as well ... another mum said having this is absolutely fantastic when you are used to having nothing ... we take it for granted but others, like, newcomers tell us what a difference it makes to the place, like they mix here from all different schools they go to here, they do things they are not allowed to do at home, with friends ... they'd be devastated to miss it ... If anything goes on or if they need help then I help.

(Mother of five, Newbald)

This section explores parents' perceptions, and those of other carers, of the play provision site in terms of how it changes not just their children's lives and their lives as parents, but also the local neighbourhood. What emerges is that:

- parents see these places as forming a crucial ingredient of their children's week – an integral experience in their daily lives
- parents recognise the mix of learning, socialising and health benefits that children can gain from these play sites
- these sites make a difference to parents' own lives too, by bringing them into contact with other parents, forming informal social bonds and support networks

- parents feel that play provision can be transformative for neighbourhoods, by cutting across social divides and creating a greater sense of community
- parents' support is often expressed through volunteering and other involvement, which in turn can be beneficial to themselves
- parents often feel that the value of these play sites is equal to, or greater than, many services for which they pay – including childcare, school trips or sports activities.

In the extract on page 47, the mother of five children, three of whom regularly attend the Newbald Church Rooms sessions, mentions many of the reasons why staffed play provision has found some of its strongest supporters among parents. These sites offer parents and carers the convenience of time apart from their children, combined with the knowledge that once there, their children are safe, in an environment that is free, mixed and social, enjoyable and beneficial for them. All of this – and it doesn't cost a thing.

Their children's week

First, the parents we spoke to emphasised the importance of these places in the average week of their children. Statements such as '[My daughter] loves it; she's very upset if she doesn't come. I just think it's great for them' (mother, Newbald) demonstrate how the sessions, even those which run only once or twice a week, are an important part of the children's daily lives. Parents also respond unambiguously about the value to the children in terms of their enjoyment and love for the place and staff – in particular, they comment about the possibilities for risk-taking in safety. This, again, is often in marked contrast to perceptions of the public realm in general, which overall aren't very positive: even in villages and small towns, many children aged 12 years or older are not allowed to walk to the staffed play setting or go to a local park alone. The perceived threat from strangers, traffic and bullying is pervasive. A grandmother-carer of two children in WCI says:

> *Yeah well it makes my life easier, I don't need to keep shouting at them for playing in the garden … well there isn't anywhere is there? There isn't any after school facilities, you'd either have to take them to the park, but there is nowhere where they can be left you know and feel safe that they are being watched. When we were kids we used to play all sorts, they just don't let them play anymore.*

For parents and carers, staffed play provision goes a long way to counteract these fears. It allows them to let their children play with other children and test boundaries in a way that would be hard either at home, at school or on the street – in a way that previous generations took for granted as a part of childhood:

> *[The rangers] make everyone feel more relaxed, and so the park gets used more, even with lots of kids with real issues – you know, they come from backgrounds with a lot of bullying, or like him his brother is in jail, and that's like a family where there is no reading and they are really struggling in school. Now the kids feel [a] lot freer with more self-confidence. They allow kids to be kids you know.*
>
> (Mother, Radstock)

This relationship is sustained by trust and communication between parents and staff, as evident when this mother says:

> *Staff important? Oh God yeah, they keep an eye on the young ones, they make sure there's more to do … plus, D— know my oldest since she was very young, I can talk to him about her.*
>
> (Mother of three children, Radstock)

Their children's lives

Parents recognise what the play provision does for their children once they're there.

> *I think it's great for the village and for the kids, for them to have somewhere to come and express themselves and learn new things. It makes her more aware of what's happening at different times of year, like they make pancakes on Pancake Day. It's given her a lot more confidence, the social activities and interacting with people. The fact that she enjoys it so much is, well, it's just great.*
>
> (Mother and committee member, Newbald)

For many parents, the sight of older children can reinforce, rather than diminish, this confidence in the site, as this mother continues:

> *A lot of the older ones have been coming for years and they still keep coming back and coming back. That proves how beneficial it is. And if the older ones got any problems, they've always got someone to talk to. It's very often difficult to talk to parents isn't it? If they've got any problems they've got somewhere to come.*

Equally, the mother of another child (4, Newbald) comments how her child:

> *says she has been looked after by the older girls which is really nice … lots of children go to different schools so this is a meeting place for the village … being part of another community outside school is*

really valuable for her, and for parents as well … we are all part of the same village after all.

A mother in Radstock puts it thus:

Yeah they feel excited they've been somewhere, even when we get home they're still full of energy from coming round but they… I feel like they're much closer to me when I get them like this, they're happier and they come home happy and it makes them feel happy and it makes me feel good.

In sum, it is a mix of the learning effects, the socialising with friends and the health benefits that come to the fore. These are recognised as crucial elements, and as aspects that can be hard for parents to provide for their children, both practically and financially, as a mother of three in Radstock comments:

If I could find other things I would but you have to pay for them and that's a great expense that's coming out. You can only do what you can afford. So it makes a great difference this kind of thing because everyone can come. I don't drive so I have to rely on transport or walking so it's tough.

A father in Manchester, talking about his son who is an only child, says:

Well if he weren't here he'd probably be on his PlayStation or his Wii, here he mixes, plays with all the kids, where we live, you know, there's not many kids his age round there really to play with. You know G— is his friend, they're inseparable, but other than that, there's no other kids. They're all older people you see where we live.

In another case this is mirrored by a mother in GAPA:

For little ones there is provision but not for this age group … there is the park but I would not send them there on their own and leave them, there is the leisure centre but you have to pay, and the swimming pool … but they can't go there on their own, you never know.

She continues to explain how it makes a difference to her child and, thereby, for herself:

For kids it really is a boost for their self-esteem which is crucial at that age, expressing themselves … staff is a key success factor, they all bring different things…. I have once said to an estate agent who was slagging off this part of Gainsborough: I wish we lived here, as there are more kids to play with here! It really makes a big difference in the life of a parent, you need somewhere else for them not just at home, something to do, confidence that you have somewhere to go, somewhere fun that you can always take them to.

Their lives as parents

The mother in GAPA, quoted above, is explicit as to how the knowledge that children have somewhere to go can improve parents' self-confidence. For many parents it goes even further, as they see many a benefit for themselves stemming from the play provision. A compelling example is the mother of three in Radstock:

Yeah well we've all got problems as parents but other parents talk to you for a bit of guidance from each other. I mean I do that, I'm a single mum with my three kids so its harder but there's lots of mums out there in the same predicament and we can talk about how it feels for us being single mums, it's hard. I moved from — and came over here and the difference here, we're all part of a team and it's great fun. When I first came here I was a bit shy about what was going to happen, but within a couple of weeks I was loving it. I thought blimey, I finally feel part of a team, part of a community. That's so nice. Like you got friends as well. Because I never had a lot of friends when I was in — it was great to get out and have friends, it felt like a family in a way. I can feel dreadful and it can cheer me up, believe it or not, I come down here and it may just be me but … the caring, I think it's the caring, the fact that you've got your own but you don't realise how much people care about each other.

Similar to the way that this mother notices the difference between this place and where she first lived, other parents are also aware that the provision from which they and their children benefit can be hard to find elsewhere. One mother of three children in Gainsborough says that, 'I looked at moving out a while ago but when I looked at other areas, like Derby or Basingstoke, there was no free out-of-school provision. GAPA and the quality of schools made all the difference, and we stayed.' Good quality play provision, in other words, becomes part of a set of key locational factors, as is also confirmed by a mother in Radstock:

It's one of the reasons we moved here in the first place – we heard about it through word of mouth, our old house was on a busy road and we wanted to move. So we saw this square and I said to my husband this is nice with the little park and then a neighbour started talking to us and told us about the play rangers, and that really made the decision for us. We parents mix a lot more when the rangers are here, it just creates this nice atmosphere, everyone is relaxed and open, otherwise people keep more to themselves really.

Their neighbourhoods

Here the mother suggests something else: not only is play provision an important factor in their daily lives, but it can change how neighbourhoods function more generally. As a mother in Newbald says: 'It is an important addition to the village, with pubs closing down and the shop in trouble, there have been so many sad changes; this is finally something positive.' Evidently, local issues vary: in Newbald it may be the decline in retail and community infrastructure, whereas in other places it might be social segregation. This is, for example, the case in Gainsborough, where a senior school nurse and parent recently started bringing her children to GAPA even though she lives elsewhere in town. She says:

> *Another role of GAPA is social integration with other kids – across class background and educational level. And because of the staff it is good contact 'cause if that was just a playground in a park, the bullies and teenagers take over, other kids would not get a look in but now all kids get a chance to play … It's becoming a Gainsborough institution through positive experiences that all parents have … it really changes perceptions of that part of town too.*

Another form of neighbourhood change is even more direct: we have already seen how in Radstock parents remarked on how the social dynamic of the park changes when the play rangers are present, and indeed this was evident on the day of our visit. An otherwise deserted park (as baseline assessments of the play rangers show, and as is the case before the arrival of the play rangers on the day of our visit) comes to life when the play rangers appear; toddlers, children and teenagers congregate as do some parents, chatting with the rangers and with each other. One mother remarks that 'we can have a street party here now' – pointing to an incipient social transformation of the neighbourhood, set within the context of what she described as:

> *lots of isolated parents in the area, lots of bad stories, crime, prison, divorce, depression … the rangers played [a] big role in the parents coming out, meeting together and creating a real network, a community feel. Parents come out who would not have before – people know each other and take care of each other now.*

Their involvement

The support of parents and carers is not only evidenced in interviews such as these but is also apparent from their active involvement in the management of these places as organisations. In many, parents or 'ex-parents' themselves are staff members; others give equipment, volunteer or are involved in the management committee. In other words, children's activities function for many parents as a catalyst for their own involvement in the setting and, through that, in the neighbourhood's affairs. In the words of one grandmother, whose children once attended GAPA and whose grandchildren now frequent it:

> *It gives me something to do. I'm retired now, but it gives me an interest. It gives me something to do apart from staying at home. Something to believe in. I'd fight tooth and nail for this place, I really would.*

In the neighbourhoods where we carried out these case studies particularly, some of which are in highly deprived wards with acute need for family support, the importance of parent involvement cannot be overstated. There are many stories of how it can be transformational in the lives of individual parents. The school nurse in Gainsborough mentions the story of one particular mother:

> *There is one mum with lots of children, they attended GAPA, she was quite depressed at some point but through contacts ended up volunteering in the shops, she feels now a lot better in the community, raised her profile, knows more people which helped her deal with mental health issues. Plus the café is well attended as is the shop, and that in an area with few other amenities is valuable too.*

Similarly, the fledgling Friends Group, which was set up for Glamis by parents, plays an important role in bringing together parents from different ethnic backgrounds. In the words of Glamis' chair: 'It's remarkable – it focuses them on what they have in common and they get on with it, creating a new understanding.'

Their assessment of value

In anticipation of a second, quantitative stage of the research (which falls beyond the scope of this report), parents were asked about their theoretical willingness to pay for what is now, without exception, free provision. This is an accepted, if not unproblematic, method for assessing the perceived value of provision, certainly in relation to other goods (Atkinson and others 2006). The approach was twofold: parents were asked whether their children attended any paid-for provision (sports, art classes, childcare, etc.), and, if so, what the cost for that was. Then parents were asked about their perception of what their child valued more, what was more important for the child, as well as what they thought their child gained from each. Then they were asked whether, in light of the answers to the questions raised, they would in theory be prepared to pay for the play provision: would they put a comparable value on it?

In parallel, and to overcome the issue of some parents not sending their children to any paid-for activity, a proxy was used: the average annual price of school trips to the average parent (around £60) as derived from a 2006 nationwide Norwich Union poll (BBC News website 16 August 2006). These questions were used as much to test the viability of willingness to pay questions as to start up a conversation about the value of play provision. Therefore the answers should be taken as anecdotal evidence rather than as hard figures, but even so, they are revealing. Some answers were very straight, going beyond the theoretical, such as this father's in Gainsborough:

> *The value of this is a lot more than school trips. This to me would come before that definitely – I mean in school trips they are walking in rows to the beach or to the museum. Well, I can take them to the beach myself, trips don't give them the freedom and interaction they get here … so I'd pay more than that, it could be £5 a week wouldn't it, per family, cause it's not a lot, but for me it would be for two children – so then it's less.*

Comparing staffed play provision to other activities seemed a logical thing to do for one mother in Newbald. When talking about one of her sons, she estimates that:

> *this would be his favourite of all things even though he loves karate and football, [which both cost £25 per month] so in a way this would be on par with these other things financially, plus you have to travel to those and stay for the whole time and you don't here … it's a good deal for so little money.*

Another mother in Gainsborough says:

> *We pay for gymnastics, £14 per month and for swimming, about £60 per year altogether or so … but she is here more often and stays longer, and there are so many more things she can do here, and there's more socialising. School trips are just no comparison. The value of this is just higher, there are always new things … £100 to £120 per year per family would be reasonable if you see what they get from it … or if you charged 50p per time probably most parents would be happy to pay.*

However, the fact that these places are free of cost is widely recognised as having inherent value, as confirmed by the view of a mother in GAPA:

Obviously, with it being free that's made a huge difference. I was paying £90 a week before for childcare, and it was no better … I think the childcare was restricted. The activities were much the same, but they were regimented in terms of what you could do, when you could do it. Here they get to pick, and if they want to do it again they can. The boys would miss being able to be outside in such a large area with so much to do. I would miss it financially.

These are, primarily, stories. Clearly, as is inevitably the case with questions about willingness to pay, the picture will be different for parents on low income – we already saw evidence of that in the previous section. Interestingly, there is some difference between the different sites in terms of what parents can imagine having to pay for. In the case of the play rangers, both in Bath and Cambridge, the question was initially met with some incredulity, understandably as the sites are in the public realm. The **value** judgement seems to stay the same however.

In sum, the research strongly suggests that parents see free play provision first and foremost as a generator of experiences for their children, rather than as provider of free childcare, even if they appreciate the ability to leave their child in good hands for however many hours a week. Their appreciation of play provision in its entirety, with all it offers children, is huge – and in some particularly poignant cases, those benefits stretch directly to their own lives. The play provision site can provide a vital support system for isolated parents, as well as represent a cornerstone of the voluntary and civic sector, creating an informal network between parents and staff and leading to greater involvement in neighbourhood affairs.

Play sites sustain a form of fast-disappearing everyday contact between neighbours, and are also important in terms of lending to the quality of the locality: research evidence shows a link between good community spirit and health outcomes; and between tightly knit communities and a positive quality of life (Buonfino and Hilder 2006).

In this context, coming together around a common cause, such as the lives of children, has been proven to have a particularly powerful effect in sustaining community cohesion across social divides: authentic engagement and participative governance affect interaction amongst users. A recent Ford Foundation project concluded that 'participation works', as taking part in tasks that belong to a shared local agenda could temporarily set aside or supersede other divisions and form a rallying point (Bach 1993). That involvement in children's lives in the daily living environment can be a very powerful source of such civic participation and social capital has been observed in recent research elsewhere (see, for example, Kapasi 2006), and the findings of this research certainly confirm this.

6   Policy partners' responses

Glamis is in the heart of the community not just geographically, it's fundamentally a different kind of place different from any public service provision – different even than public sector adventure playgrounds. The ethos is key, public sector provision inevitably needs to be run within constraints; the council is very Every Child Matters-driven by necessity: safeguarding children and achievement. Glamis provides a different kind of experience – more permissive, there is more freedom, and that difference in culture is a strength. It complements the mainstream, I am not saying that every place should be like that but it is good it exists. Compared to other provision around here, which is now mostly school-based with Extended Schools, it's good to get out, to go somewhere that's not about schools, but only about being active with other children.
(Local area partnership manager, Glamis)

This section provides an overview of how a wide range of stakeholders view the role of staffed play provision and how they view discussions about its impact on children's lives and beyond. What emerges is that:

● there are clear indications of changing times – the importance of play provision is increasingly being recognised by a range of policy-makers and public service stakeholders
● policy partners recognise the crucial role of staff in expanding the range of play opportunity for children and young people
● policy partners value play for a mix of intrinsic and instrumental reasons – whilst emphasising the right to play for its own sake, they are very aware of the difference that play provision make to their work in terms of, for example, safety and anti-social behaviour, and the use of parks and social capital
● there is no agreement about the best way to capture such benefits – whilst quantitative outcome measuring is seen as a necessity by some, others emphasise the need to improve output data (attendance and uptake) or see untapped potential in using qualitative accounts by communicating the children's own stories.

Changing times

What was immediately evident was the wide acknowledgement of changing times. Recent investment is marked not just through the availability of funds but also in the changed attitudes of decision-makers and the general public.

Times are changing. Councillors are getting the message about free play and playable space. It's now accepted that play is a generally good thing in itself, which on the one hand – yes – contributes to concerns that matter to the Council, and that's important, but primarily is a good thing intrinsically. It's largely thanks to the government investment – we now have Councillors competing over new investment!

These remarks by a deputy director of Children's Services reflect the change in recent times. Our interviews suggest how, increasingly, the benefits of play are being understood, including by those outside the play world. A Bath and North East Somerset district councillor for Radstock mentions a wide range of benefits:

It's a health generator, works on the obesity agenda, and is psychologically important too, to be away from the computer at least for a bit and have adventures outside ... children have ultra-protected lives, they need a sense of space, having fun instead of pressure – the endless striving to succeed can go too far nowadays ... no, for me it is not at all difficult to defend play at the moment, certainly with the government's £235m.

It is clear that the evidence gathered over recent years by the play sector has reached a key audience at the local level.

The role of staffing

Within this general understanding, staffed play provision is seen to be particularly valuable. The same district councillor continues:

staff is crucial – their training and abilities make the difference. There has been a real short-sightedness of play policies: making playworkers redundant is a great mistake. Time to play with children is now rare – parents don't have time anymore ... that's why play rangers are so important ... they can show this generation of parents the confidence of playing outside, to which parents are not accustomed anymore. Also play rangers fulfil the role previously fulfilled by uniformed organisations like scouts, forming role models, showing new things – so yes we want our money in local play rangers, not in faraway leisure centres – especially as many parents here cannot afford to take their children to Bath or Bristol.

In Newbald, this is reflected by the parish council chair, who comments that 'parents are neurotic about the public realm nowadays. Kids have nowhere to go, especially in cold winters, and with a largely car-driven place where it's hard for them to move around, they need somewhere warm, inside, and staffed.' And a community development officer for Cambridge City Council says that:

Play rangers are actually a really cost-effective way of plugging provision gaps; the problem with fixed play is, it is only for certain age groups and it only interests them for a certain time. Staffed play can do much more, it intensifies all the benefits and provides a link function for those who want to get involved in sport, in coaching, in the arts ... a referral service. What this does is create a focus for play, children really seem to converge on this, they get introduced to others and do things they would not otherwise do ... ordinary play equipment is quite limited often, and some of the public spaces quite bleak, so this really creates a different experience – and therefore the recs get used a lot better. I have seen recs with children of different ages together, networking between parents especially for new parents and with pre-school kids. ... It might even have a residual effect beyond when they are there: it might create ideas, encourage risk-taking, focus on natural play.

And in Bath and North East Somerset, the strategic play officer argues that one of the important contributions the play rangers can make is in changing negative attitudes towards children and young people: 'Segregation between ages is the key problem. Our aim is to give kids choices, for them to move freely through the neighbourhood and be respected in [the] community ... the rangers facilitate that.'

Interpretation of value

Both policy-makers and frontline practitioners tend to speak about a mix of intrinsic and instrumental value. To them, the instrumental value lies in what staffed play provision does both to change the lives of children and have a wider impact – but it is all part of the same story. A clear example is the perception of a police constable in Radstock who, after speaking about the decrease in anti-social behaviour, and the difference this has made to parks as a result of increased play provision, emphasises that:

First and foremost they have the right to play near home, not somewhere faraway – politicians seem to want to put money into expensive swimming pools and adult facilities but we need our play and youth work on the streets here. It is not a privilege it is a right.

This recognition goes hand in hand with recognition of the difference it makes to his daily work. Together with neighbourhood policing, the play rangers have changed local dynamics:

> *It is very positive – we have no issues with that age group in Tyning whereas we do have issues elsewhere … this reflects the work of the rangers here: less damage, less anti-social behaviour. I've been 33 years in the police force; I have seen a big change in kids' and parents' behaviour, there's much better contact now, and better interaction. I enjoy going to work now – I could have retired 3 years ago … our problems with CYP [children and young people] have been resolved to a degree, when compared to the dark days a decade ago when youth work had closed and places were barren.*

Staffed play provision is seen as strongly positive on another agenda. One Head of Open Spaces for a district council argues, after having listed a series of intrinsic benefits to children, that:

> *from my perspective anything that uses spaces, that educates people that public spaces are there to be enjoyed and valued, that maximises their utility, is good. It also means more eyes and ears, more sense of ownership, less vandalism. It's both the energy and safety that emanates from a park when you walk by and it's used like that, you feel it must be safe because children are playing here.*

He confirms the reality that there is a long way to go before his vision is true – but having staff outdoors might be a key way to get there. Ideally he would like play rangers to work with schools as well – 'get schools out of their grounds!' – and maximise that benefit.

Equally, a leisure and parks manager for Manchester City Council, involved in the Parktastic project co-delivered by WCI, describes how this programme helps to break through the persistently negative safety perceptions about Manchester parks, thereby increasing parents' and children's confidence to go out and use the parks; she cites the work of the government's Commission for Architecture and the Built Environment (CABE) on 'parkforces' and mentions how the play ranger projects essentially help to deliver on this (CABE 2005).

However, she feels there is more to it: the presence of play rangers also leads to parents getting involved in delivering sessions and creating links with existing Friends groups of different parks. A trend towards wider civic engagement with parks is thereby intensified and given a more explicit children and young people's angle, which is sometimes lacking from the work of Friends groups.

So you get more interesting forms of participation, connecting different groups in neighbourhoods, and that leads to improved social cohesion in parks beyond the play session itself – it really has a regenerative impact on the neighbourhood, even though we don't track that formally we see it happen: it helps people in the neighbourhood to apply for grants, fosters community ownership, [and] builds civic capacity.

There are many such examples of how policy stakeholders see the play provision sites and their programmes as crucial to the very fabric of the local area, and how this is connected to the nature of the provision. The local area partnership manager in Tower Hamlets says:

You know, Glamis is a great example of local management and that's a salient argument in itself – very relevant in a place like this. Pride in place and protection for children at the same time, that's great – you know, different people come together here in a way that's different than anywhere else in the area and which is not at all easy in Tower Hamlets – classes and races mix, they are really successful at that and put a lot of effort in – I would say they are particularly successful in Glamis … and that is really because of the magical experience that children have, it makes them come back across a divide. For a Council provision it would be difficult to reproduce that sense of ownership.

The local police constable in the ward where Glamis is located agrees:

It goes without saying for me. If you provide things to do and kids are occupied then yes, anti-social behaviour will go down. There seem to be less anti-social behaviour calls on that estate than elsewhere and I do think it's definitely linked to Glamis … and not just crime: there is also a better sense of community, parents go pick up their kids talk to each other and find common ground … there's the possibility then to do more community events, get involved.

This clearly confirms the findings of the previous section about the importance and potential of civic participation.

In other words, support for the practice of play provision comes from a range of stakeholders for a large number of reasons – which, whilst acknowledging the intrinsic benefits of play, touch directly upon the heart of the government agenda regarding the public realm, volunteering and social capital.

Measuring output

One of the frequent topics of discussion among stakeholders was the issue of policy and project evaluation and the use of outcome or output indicators. Here, the story is widely divergent in terms of what is being measured, and how and to what end it is being measured.

Basically, stakeholders mentioned three positions.

The first position emphasises the need to measure **outcome** in order to make a long-term case beyond the current funding rounds, and some stakeholders are working towards measures for doing so (e.g., Cambridge and Bath and North East Somerset Council are currently working on different types of outcome evaluation frameworks). However, many of those who would advocate this in principle emphasise that the level of data and staff resources available are currently insufficient to work towards this ambition. One example is the district manager in Manchester who says:

> *Staff resources on performance are limited; it would be beneficial if we had guidance on this but even then, the data available isn't detailed enough.*

An early years and extended services manager confirms this:

> *We have the ambition yes but Local Area Partnership level data is not good enough, schools and Children's Centre data are fine but for example, our Primary Care Trust data don't have a usable format … we will start on a limited level, with Play Pathfinder work, ex-ante and ex-post evaluations, and generate our own data.*

A police constable in Radstock has no illusions about the effect of quantitative measuring of what is most important to him:

> *We cannot distinguish reporting logs on anti-social behaviour per age range so we cannot prove the effect this work [the play rangers] has, one over-21 nightclub audience could change the whole picture in the stats.*

Some mention that, despite the ambition being valuable, 'it would be too big a price to pay if it impacts on play quality itself, even though it would be beneficial if a method was found' (leisure and parks manager, Manchester). Others are more vocal about the limits. One deputy director of Children's Services asserts that, after a similar exercise on the impact of youth provision, she feels that:

*measuring in detail the effects on children's health, socialising ...
that way madness lies. It's unnecessary and the resource
implications are simply huge.*

The second position emphasises the strengthening of **output**
measurement as a necessary first step to show that improved
investment is widening access and uptake of existing and future play
provision capacity. The argument is that, with a positive outcome being
accepted and after asserting that detailed outcome measurement is
impossible or undesirable, we should focus on what might be feasible:
for example, tracking the number and percentage of children within an
area that actually use a facility. This is currently already happening in
some places. For example lottery-funded projects, such as
Manchester's Parktastic, already produce quantitative output
indicators.

It is a part of good practice for all six case studies, who tend to see
this as burdensome yet inevitable, and who have all put simple
protocols in place to achieve this.

But many play and open space stakeholders report that, for example,
recording of attendance in parks and play centres is patchy or absent,
so there needs to be a drive to achieve this first – especially, as some
remark, for third sector delivery partners who need to improve in this
area.

No one suggests, of course, that the output measure alone should
define the success of the provision; such assessments do not do
justice to the richness and variety of services and experiences.
However, as one ingredient of a broader impact framework, it needs to
be taken seriously.

The third position is the emphasis on **qualitative stories** and the
experience of frontline professionals, and some stakeholders see
untapped potential in using qualitative accounts of impact much more
creatively. This primarily consists of communicating stories about
children and how they change, especially stories by the children
themselves. For example, one director of Children's Services says that
'in a Council scrutiny session I was pleased to be asked by a Councillor
for real stories, qualitative case studies rather than quantitative
data'.

This is confirmed by a strategic play officer, who mentions that
'instead of number-crunching, I do case studies which I find particularly
useful when I have to convince the powers that be that there needs to
be more attention given to play rangers'. She argues that, for example,

when the play rangers' input enables vulnerable children to access services, which in turn might lead to behaviour change, this is best captured in narrative.

Equally, the local police constable for Glamis, when talking about how the changes in the area relate to the adventure playground, says:

> *I don't always need to go by figures because the perception is clear, from what I see and from what people on the street say to me: the area is better for it.*

Others mention that qualitative measuring, such as focus groups with parents, needs to play an important role alongside output measure. In Cambridge, the Head of Community Development of the council explains:

> *How do we showcase it? That's a mix: opening opportunities for kids to demonstrate the value of what they do with us to the community; events, with CDs and videos of performances … we are a small city after all; if councillors see the kids enjoy themselves, that makes a huge difference.*

In fact many comment that mixing methods is crucial: output indicators combined with focus groups, National Indicator data (gathered through schools) and perception questionnaires – grouped together, these will provide a reliable and persuasive picture. Similarly, a leisure and parks manager in Manchester cautions against an over-reliance on 'hard' data.

> *We should also trust the professional judgement of playworkers more as basis for evaluation, lots of playworkers feel they should provide play not measure.*

In other words, the discussion about measuring is ongoing, and for many stakeholders is becoming more urgent in the context of the current round of investment and for future change based around the commissioning of new projects. Enrique Peñalosa, the charismatic reformer and ex-Mayor of Bogotá in Colombia, famously said that: 'Children are a kind of indicator species. If we can build a successful city for children, we will have a successful city for all people' (Peñalosa and Ives 2002), and this belief is increasingly shared by service providers and others. How to capture this is a challenge indeed, and one which we will return to in the following chapters.

7   Institutional links

The previous section shows how different stakeholders across a wide range of key policy fields see the value of play, both because they acknowledge the intrinsic value it holds and because they see how it helps them deliver on their core professional objectives. The links between play and wider policy outcomes were already highlighted in the Demos report *Seen and Heard* (Beunderman, Hannon and Bradwell 2007), which advocated stronger linkages between the play world and the healthy neighbourhood, the sustainable transport movement and other related agenda.

We have already seen how in many cases staffed play provision forms a focus for local volunteering and for personalised contact between the public, third sector organisations and policy stakeholders. But this goes further, in two ways. First, and as shown above, in many cases it is **staffed** provision that makes the important difference, in a way that play provision in the public realm alone cannot. Second, and as we will show here, there are many examples of staffed play provision being increasingly recognised, on an institutional level, as a vital element of multi-agency working. This happens in five distinct ways.

1. By providing holistic services to young people: staffed play provision fills a gap between statutory early years and youth provision.
2. By providing a touchpoint: for the engagement of children and young people, improving relations and encouraging children to make a positive contribution to their area.
3. By capacity building: making links with other service providers, such as the police and parks staff, who recognise a need to increase their understanding of play and children.
4. By resource sharing: play provision sites often share staff, space and on-the-ground knowledge resources with others in the third sector, acting as important local cornerstones of service delivery.
5. Through individual approaches to children: locally, play provision sites can be an important stakeholder in safeguarding children in need and in providing support to their families.

A youth worker in Tower Hamlets describes a typical situation that clearly illustrates the value of play provision within the services offered by the council:

There is a service gap between the early years service and youth service: there is no statutory service for the 8–13 age group. Glamis bridges that gap; it is a bolt-on service, additional to what we do. So now we can work together and offer a holistic service to all ages in

facilitating early stage engagement of children and young people in that process. Similarly, working with third sector organisations to deliver projects such as Manchester's Parktastic scheme shows how capacity and capability can be built over time. A play development officer for Manchester City Council says:

> *Parktastic helps joint working with wardens, getting them to change routines and do playwork. This implies a fundamental culture change in that sector – which can be hard but worth it. How park wardens and how Friends groups see play is changing as a result.*

These institutional links are embedded in a wider trend towards stronger community working, empowering those in frontline service delivery and collaborative working, as encompassed by the government's 'double devolution' agenda. As such they are an integral part of joined-up government, delivering change locally, working on concerns at the heart of the social fabric in neighbourhoods (CLG 2008; Parker and Bartlett 2008).

Some of this points to the fourth way for institutional growth: the important issue of sharing resources. Glamis, WCI and GAPA are to some degree combined children's and family centres or, at least the case Glamis, offer their spaces for joint working. For example, a Sure Start coordinator for Gainsborough explains how GAPA has obtained funding for a crèche, leading to increased collaboration:

> *We share staff resources, they have trained up our staff for free on some of our programmes, we have outreach meetings in their building … it is partnership working at its best I think – and that helps a lot in what we do. And it's not just with us that they work: they run storytelling sessions at the local library, and work in the local park on den building to attract kids and parents, they work together with Friends group, so that all get involved in play, which creates a really nice atmosphere in the park, and on play days in the summer.*

The staff, space and organisational resources of GAPA are put to work throughout Gainsborough. Similarly, a senior sports development officer in Cambridge Council emphasises how ChYpPS has been crucial in getting a sports development programme called *Street Games* off the ground:

> *ChYpPS know the kids and areas intimately, they bring important stuff to the table, have a link function to sport – you could not run a programme like that without ChYpPS and their networks, knowledge, they know what children and young people want … that's where the beauty of working together comes in, we can help each other.*

Even more succinctly, a Greenspace officer of the same council says: 'They are our eyes and ears … one of our key objectives generally is to make people feel comfortable in parks and commons and offer as many different experiences as possible – they help achieve that.'

A last role is connected to all four ways mentioned above, and goes to the heart of institutional strengthening taking place throughout our case studies. It is the ability to work around individual children and their families where there is a need. As a senior school nurse in Gainsborough says:

GAPA comes to Child in Need meetings around individual kids (together with the social worker, school teacher, nurse). Their role is absolutely important here locally; children who need child protection plans, as part of that we send them to GAPA if they don't go already – it gives them socialisation outside school, increased confidence, gives families a break in large households. There are six of those kids currently at GAPA. It gives them a safe environment with adults and we can work around behaviour issues.

A senior organiser for Homestart, the family support charity, emphasises this local role:

We aim to support families with children undergoing stressful or difficult situations. We refer people to them and they to us. It's very personal … we work together on a local Credit Union to keep people out of the hands of loan sharks. I'd do anything to support this playground, I think it does a great job.

This is not just the case in GAPA, as evident from these comments from Cambridge's Head of Community Development:

ChYpPS are our first point of contact for parents who want to engage with the council generally, on a wide range of issues about anti-social behaviour but also housing … it pioneers other forms of working with the public generally. Some of the most powerful impacts are around referred children and their parents, where the Reccy Rangers have a linking and referring role for people who would otherwise often feel that the Council is remote and hard to approach, and keeping informal contact subsequently … the uniform that the rangers wear is important, it gives confidence, consistency, a sense of quality, and breeds trust.

A community worker in Abbey Ward confirms:

The parents are a lot happier on days with rangers there to have their kids go there. Especially in this ward there is some

*resentment, feelings that nobody in the Council cares about us, so
the Council having a presence, coming out, is so important.*

These issues go to the core of recent discussions about public service
provision and service design, which have focused on the interface
between service users and providers, and what citizens experience as
they move through public services such as the care system. Using user
journeys and qualitative accounts, these discussions shed light on the
often illogical, impersonal ways in which such services are organised
and the negative impact this has on crucial public goods, such as trust
in the council. It seems that, as natural hubs for children and parents,
play provision sites play a role in humanising and personalising public
service provision through giving council service provision a
recognisable face; and through the cross-agency links and joint
working methods forged by frontline delivery staff from across the
public and third sector (Heapy and Parker 2005, Bartlett and
Leadbeater 2008).

Ultimately, this leads us back to the government's core policies for
children and young people and to local authority and neighbourhood
policy delivery, as captured in, respectively, the Every Child Matters
framework, launched in 2003, and the new performance framework for
local authorities and its National Indicator Set, which has been in
operation since April 2008. From the wide-ranging account given in the
seven sections of this chapter, a narrative emerges that points to a
range of benefits and outcomes even though what matters first and
foremost is the ability of children to engage in diverse forms of play.

It is possible to link those benefits directly with the Every Child
Matters framework, for example, by pointing to:

- the valuable outdoor activity for children who might otherwise stay
  in (Be Healthy)
- the refuge offered to children with difficult home situations and
  nowhere else to go, and the increased potential to link individual
  children and families to particular safeguarding services by
  providing yet another, personalised interface (Stay Safe)
- the sheer richness and variety of play opportunity offered across a
  wide age range, and to the way this complements other services and
  the offer of the public realm, as well as to the myriad learning
  moments that occur in this process that encourage children to
  shape their own learning (Enjoy and Achieve)
- the diverse ways in which children and young people get actively
  involved in changing the physical environment of these 'children's
  spaces' or even in their management, thus enhancing their sense of
  agency and self-confidence (Making a Positive Contribution)

- the fact that these places are free and open to all children in neighbourhoods where this often matters a lot to parents (Achieving Economic Well-being).

Equally, they can be directly linked to many of the 188 new National Indicators for Local Authorities and Local Authority Partnerships, some of which capture the Every Child Matters outcomes but many of which go beyond. In Bath and North East Somerset, this link is being made in a draft Play Pathfinder evaluation framework.

However, the full value of staffed play provision cannot easily be captured in such indicators. The next chapter will further reflect on this issue.

Image: Newbald Church Rooms Young People's Project

This research focused on the benefits and value of free, staffed play provision. The study aimed to find ways to capture and communicate the full extent of what can be achieved in good quality play provision for the benefit of children first and foremost, but also for young people, parents, and their communities. The study focused on producing a qualitative evidence base from observations and stories collected at the six case study sites. This chapter builds on the findings, reflecting on the issue of capturing *value*.

What is evident is the extraordinary complexity of value derived from this kind of provision, and the huge diversity of ways in which it is created. There is extensive literature on the different benefits that varied play experiences bring. The evidence in this study points overwhelmingly to one thing: good quality *staffed* play provision plays a crucial role in increasing the affordances to engage in such rich and varied play, and particularly the kinds of play that are limited or endangered elsewhere, such as risk in play. In this way, staffed play provision can expand upon the possibilities of, and to an extent compensate for, the individual child's often limited experiences in the general public realm or in institutional sites such as schools.

The case studies in this research cut across a range of organisational forms and settings: we studied adventure playgrounds, play centres and play ranger projects. Moreover, they cut across a range of organisational set-ups: from a local authority-funded and -delivered programme (the Cambridge ChYpPS rangers); to a local authority-initiated and -funded, but third sector delivered, project (Bath and North East Somerset play rangers); to projects initiated by the third sector (Newbald Church Rooms, GAPA, WCI and Glamis Adventure Playground). All of them rely on a mix of funding: from local authority and Big Lottery Fund grants for specific programmes; to self-generated income such as voluntary contributions or small-scale entrepreneurial activities; to donations in kind – often time. Whilst it would be worthwhile to analyse in more detail how play setting type and organisational set-ups might impact on the effectiveness of these places in creating settings for free play, that was not the key task in this research. Rather, we focus on what they have in common.

We suggest three ways of explaining what these examples of good practice have in common, and why this matters for evaluating the impact of play. These ways are:

- emphasising the importance of 'software' (staff attitudes, site culture, etc.) rather than 'hardware' (built elements)
- using the play value triangle, a modified version of the cultural value triangle alluded to in Chapter 2, which has been developed by Demos research in the cultural sector and which will be explained below
- emphasising the use of storytelling as a communication strategy.

Hardware and software

Staffed play provision should not be seen, primarily, as 'hardware' providing physical sites and spaces for play, but as 'setting a setting' or creating 'software' – a site-specific culture, atmosphere and enabling infrastructure for engaging in play. This is what children say and display in their behaviour; it is what staff strive to achieve and see as their core mission; it is something that parents recognise and value, and it is recognised by policy-makers and community stakeholders, including those who work beyond the play sector.

That good quality staffed play provision goes beyond a physical infrastructure is most potently shown by play ranger projects, which have no fixed physical setting. By creating a social and cultural setting they bring the public realm to life. Therefore, if we only focus on the 'hardware' of staffed play provision we would miss the point of what goes on in these places.

In these sites, the staff establish a series of protocols – covering the spatial atmosphere, safety, behaviour rules, and the offering of suggestions and help – that establish the character of the site as playful, as a 'children's place' that functions in a way that the streets, parks, unstaffed playgrounds and schools currently do not (Moss and Petrie 2002). It is these series of subtle protocols, stemming from the Playwork Principles and a sympathetic understanding of children and play, that make parents confident and give children the freedom to experiment, take risks, meet friends and confront physical or social challenges; and thereby bring about the seven Best Play outcomes (Children's Play Council, National Playing Fields Association and Playlink 2000) and the creation of 'capabilities', Amartya Sen's and Martha Nussbaum's (1993) positive freedoms.

By focusing on the rights of children to free, supported, self-motivated and varied play, these places create benefits for adults too. Importantly, it is the 'software', not the hardware alone, that enables parents to feel confident, meet, exchange stories and worries, find new ideas and possibly links to other support services. This is how parents value play provision – not as some form of free childcare but as a way of generating experiences for their children and as a source of mental, moral and practical support for themselves. And the benefits are not just limited to what directly concerns them as parents, but also to them as local residents: it makes the neighbourhood a better, safer and more rewarding place to be.

This emphasis on play spaces as 'children's places' mirrors ongoing research about the public realm generally, where there has been increasing scepticism about the often taken-for-granted ability of physical public *spaces* to bring people together, encourage sociability across social divisions and, eventually, generate prized outcomes such as trust and social cohesion. In reality, as the geographer Ash Amin has put it, 'the micro-cultures of space matter' – and they are created not just by financial largesse for physical sites, but by careful thinking about their location, design, management, programming and adaptability. Crucial to this is not just the squares and streets that make up what is formally called 'public space', but also public services and community spaces, the so-called 'parochial domain' (Amin 2007, 2002, Beunderman and Lownsbrough 2007). In fact, play provision can be compared to public institutions such as libraries, which, like the play sector, have recently seen renewed attention, interest and investment, as well as critical appraisal. For play provision to function optimally in a changing world with the changing and diverse needs of users, we need to invest in people, organisational and partnership networks, and in innovation in the protocols that allow them to function – not just in buildings (Beunderman and Lownsbrough 2007, Holden and Jones 2006).

Understanding this is the real challenge involved in animating and activating the public realm – bringing it to life beyond the mere provision of pavements and ornamental planting – a task now the subject of attention from both the public and third sector. (Initiatives such as Streets Alive, the CLG-funded Street Games programme and the CABE publication *Parks Need Parkforce* (2005) discuss such issues in more detail.) It is a complex task as it points to a need for a culture change in the way we conceive public realm projects, away from the current often negative attitude to children and young people within the public realm and towards something more positive.

Finally the children interviewed for this research come from a wide range of backgrounds. Some of them evidently live challenging lives; whilst others displayed great happiness and confidence with regard to the playground as well to their everyday lives at home, their neighbourhoods and the other opportunities they have to play, in clubs, on holiday or even at school. From their words and behaviour it is clear that both groups value very highly the play opportunity offered by the study sites. Staffed, free play provision offers a complementary experience that adds to what, for some children and young people, are already richly endowed lives; for others, it is a lifeline without which they would struggle. In either case, much of the difference is made by the personal relations with staff – the software – whether directly through help, suggestions, conversations, facilitating play or helping to generate ideas, or indirectly through just providing the setting, the atmosphere and a sense of safety.

Capturing value

To understand and communicate such value, much debate has focused on the respective merits of emphasising the intrinsic or the instrumental value of play, as well as on ways of quantifying any measurable benefits. However, **capturing** is not the same as measuring.

This is the core focus of the Demos research on cultural value (Holden 2004, 2006). In an analogy to the cultural value triangle (see page 76), it would appear from our research that a similar triangle is valid for the benefits that staffed play provision bring. This triangle would contain the following elements.

Intrinsic values – the most crucial and immediate set of values, these are explicitly non-economic, derived from rich and varied, self-determined play. Intrinsic values are the set of values that relate to the subjective experience of play, intellectual, emotional and spiritual. Because these are experienced at the level of the individual they are difficult to articulate in terms of mass 'outcomes'. However, this is not just a version of 'art for art's sake' – many of Martha Nussbaum's core capabilities fit into this category, as they emphasise positive freedoms that enable human beings to live a fuller life, and not simply one for the instrumental benefit of society. But, as John Holden puts it: 'Intrinsic values are better thought of then as the *capacity and potential* [of culture, or play] to affect us, rather than as measurable and fixed stocks of worth' (2006: 15).

In the staffed play provision studied here, the intrinsic value created is evident in the increased opportunity for play, through: reaching more children who would otherwise have lesser quality experiences outside the home and school or who would not be able to leave the home for leisure time at all; giving children greater confidence to play and experiment in safety increasing the range of play opportunities offered; animating the public realm in the case of play ranger work; and through contributing to a wider cultural change in the public realm in the long term.

Instrumental values – these relate to the ancillary effects of play, where play is seen to contribute to wider social or economic objectives. As Chapter 2 shows, this kind of value has been examined in various studies that document the economic and social significance of investing in play provision. They mostly focus on particular aspects, but rarely produce cost estimates. This study shows the sheer variety of benefits created, enabled or intensified through staffed play provision, even beyond their impact on children. These include providing volunteering opportunities, unlocking physical improvement in public spaces, improving race relations and decreasing anti-social behaviour. Not all of these can or should be captured in figures or our National Indicators, let alone in monetary terms. Indeed, what is striking is the number of stakeholders who mention that qualitative accounts are as powerful or valid, in their personal opinion and in their experience with decision-makers, as quantitative measurements.

Institutional values – these relate to the processes and techniques that organisations adopt working to create play opportunities. We suggest a more practical definition of institutional value than the more conceptual one of 'public value'. Based on the use of the term in Demos' cultural value work, this focuses on the networks created by staffed play providers and the opportunities that such 'institutional thickness' bring to create additional value. This could be the enhancing of efficiency through complementarity or being able to work around individual children and their needs together with partners. What is then created is a coherent ecology of children's places and children's services. Sometimes called 'orgware', this represents the ability of institutional processes in organisations to respond to challenges.

Working collaboratively is an important aspect in playing this role successfully and, in turn, it works to create 'public value': increased trust from citizens in each other and in public or third sector institutions; improved access to services; greater transparency and fairness; and more responsiveness to feedback from the public. Our study has found very powerful accounts of how staffed play provision is creating such values in practice.

The 'value triangle' is shown in Figure 1 below.

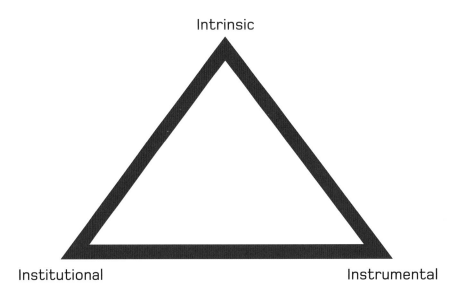

Figure 1: The 'value triangle'
Source: Holden, J (2006) *Cultural Value and the Crisis of Legitimacy*. London: Demos.

John Holden argues that the values in this I–I–I (Intrinsic, Instrumental, Institutional) triangle are played out in a second triangular relationship between professionals, politicians/policy-makers and the public. This is akin to Lester and Russell's (2008) analysis of the 'tension field' between policy, literature and practice. The overlapping triangles of I–I–I and P-P-P (Professionals, Politicians and policy-makers, the Public, see Figure 2) will always be a subject of discussion. By making the values explicit we can rationalise the discussion, *and* also realise that without the creation of intrinsic benefits, the other two values will be moot. As we will argue in our Conclusion, the crucial difference between the cultural sector and the play sector is that, whilst some politicians and other stakeholders seem to have accepted the principled case for intrinsic value in play much more than was the case in the cultural sector, upon publication of *Cultural Value and the Crisis of Legitimacy* (Holden 2006), the relationship with the public sector and the play sector is still underdeveloped.

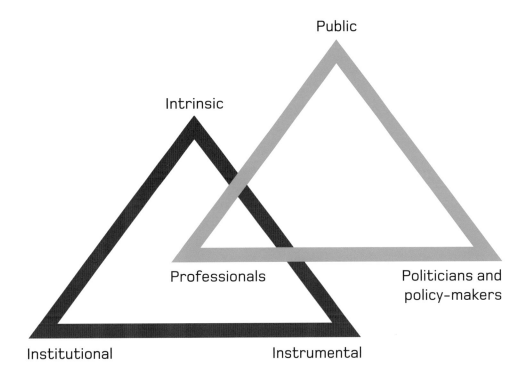

Figure 2: Overlapping triangles

Source: Holden, J (2006) *Cultural Value and the Crisis of Legitimacy*. London: Demos.

Telling the story

Our research suggests that fully capturing the value of play might imply a need to pay more attention to the innate potential of the play sector by scaling up the approach permeating this report: to tell the stories of children's own experiences and those of parents and others involved. Using storytelling as an approach to policy accountability or organisational practice might have been viewed with doubt in the past, but recent trends across the public and private sectors means that, increasingly, the power of stories is being taken seriously. A recent Demos publication on public engagement in the city of Glasgow, *The Dreaming City* (Hassan, Mean and Tims 2007), noted why this is an empowering development: the power to tell stories is innate – everyone can do it, and it generates a type of knowledge that people can relate to beyond specialist professional skills or bureaucratic procedures. Therefore it is particularly effective in its ability to connect with people generally, which, as the Conclusion to this report will argue, will increasingly be crucial (see also Simmons 2006).

The Dreaming City goes on to note that 'recently, storytelling has been embraced and championed as the must-have tool in a wide range of fields, from savvy businesses to efficient medical practices'. It quotes the author Annette Simons, who puts it even more strongly: 'People don't want information. They are up to their eyeballs in information. They want faith – faith in you, your goals, your success, in the story you tell. It is faith that moves mountains not facts. Facts do not give birth to faith. Faith needs a story to sustain it' (Hassan, Mean and Tims 2007: 68). The rise of storytelling can be seen in this context, of trying to find pathways to simply and honestly explain an increasingly complex, messy world. Fisher (1987) argues that this shift amounts to the emergence of a 'new story paradigm'.

Within the play sector, many organisations already use such creative evaluation and communication practices. Barnardo's *Evaluation of the Tower Hamlets Community Play Programme*, for example, used 'write and draw' techniques, inspired by and adapted from Action for Sick Children's research into healthcare, which argues that such creative techniques are 'an accepted way of discovering children's knowledge and views through inviting them to produce pictures with words and captions' (Creegan and others 2004: 20).

Another good example is the Torbay Children's Fund Play Roadshow DVD, produced by a group of young people, aged 9–17, who called themselves FUNK (Film Us Now Krew) and who were supported by participation workers from the Children's Society Take Part Participation Project. The DVD project looked at the impact of the Children's Fund play services and has five short sections: How has it made a difference?; What do the kids think?; Having fun; What do the adults think?; and What do the officials have to say? The children involved learned about the Every Child Matters outcomes by, as one of them put it:

> *playing games and doing silly stuff ... we thought about how we have fun and how going along ... makes us feel healthy and stuff. We made collages about the five outcomes and wrote down things about the projects that were important to us ... we learnt how to interview people and how to use a video camera. We worked on our own interview questions, all to do with the five outcomes, because we wanted to find out how children feel about things.*
> (Torbay Children's Fund Annual Report 2005/06)

The wider impact of using this approach with children was evident in the development of the Torbay Play Strategy: the mainstreaming of Children's Fund play services; the creation of two new play development posts within the local authority; and in the securing of funding for voluntary play organisations. The use of the DVD to illustrate how children felt about their play services was hugely influential with officers and politicians; as Steven Chown from Play England informs us, a commitment to the play strategy is included in the Community Plan, Children and Young People's Plan and Mayor's Vision.

Working creatively with children and young people to communicate the rich stories that already exist is proven to be effective. Such techniques tend to be popular with children and young people also, as is evident, for example, in the many successful youth radio programmes across the United Kingdom and the increasingly creative engagement with online media (Bradwell, Hannon and Tims 2008). Noted also was the eager willingness with which many of the children responded to the questions we asked for this report. The will to tell stories is innate. It also forms an effective way to access the wider public's play memories, tapping into the fact that all adults, even those without children, will have play stories. Accessing such memories is a powerful way to connect with the wider public and increase understanding of the importance of play.

The reporting and communication practices in our case studies vary; while some primarily (and with success) use evaluation and community surveys to communicate with funders or to evaluate services and improve the offer internally, others generate higher profile outreach material to communicate with parents and children. In particular, Glamis, GAPA and the Cambridge ChYpPS have developed attractive illustrated material that tells the story of what goes on in their services in different ways. However, rarely are they able to develop a more deliberate communication strategy that informs the public not just of what is on offer, but also why this offer is important and what difference it can make. This is not because the knowledge isn't there, as it is clear from our research that playworkers are instinctively able to observe and capture this potential as part of their reflexive practice. It is, first and foremost, a resourcing issue. As the play ranger manager of Wandsdyke Play Association in Radstock says:

> *I would love to be able to sit down and write down the stories I know – and there are many, about individual children and young people, about their experiences about how their lives have changed. I think all playworkers know such stories and it would be so motivating to make more of them. It's finding the time really – and being supported and validated in the notion that this is a valuable way of reporting.*

This response is typical: with stretched resources, the existing duties of researching and compiling data for funders is already a burden for these organisations. Therefore, even though there is the will, spending more time on an additional communication task seems daunting. However, given that such narrative knowledge is already implicitly held by playworkers, making it explicit by spreading the stories to a wider audience would certainly be a worthwhile effort, and one that will appeal more to many playworkers than the predominantly quantitative effort often required of them at present.

Image: Wythenshawe Community Initiative

A second step in this research commission was originally to push towards a quantitative outcome evaluation of play provision. We see significant issues in achieving this. The value of staffed play provision cannot easily be captured through statistics – in part because of the intangible nature of much of play and its benefits, but also because of the complex contribution it makes to other agenda, ranging, as we have seen, from the government's ambitions for volunteering and third sector capacity-building to the combating of anti-social behaviour to improving the 'interface' between service provider and service user in social services (for more information see the Office for the Third Sector website accessed 4 November 2008, and Heapy and Parker 2005).

There are a number of general methodological points to be made here.

- Establishing a causal link between play provision and a beneficial economic or social outcome is difficult because the benefits may not be immediately apparent, differing geographical boundaries, the context in which it takes place and the multiplicity of other factors impacting on the result.

- The existing literature on benefit and outcome is often specific to time and place, leading to issues around 'benefit transfer': the question as to how the attributed effects can be transferred from one context to another (Atkinson and others 2006).

- There is little in the way of longitudinal evidence to support correlation between play provision and its effects because play provision practice, the context in which it takes place, and policy goals are constantly shifting.

- It is virtually impossible to prove that, even if a particular play provision project or programme intervention works, this is the most direct and cost-effective way of achieving a particular social or economic aim.

- Usage statistics of play provision settings vary in consistency and quality, although there have been improvements recently.

- Available data regarding outcomes for children and young people, parents and the wider community are partial (data are not available for the full range of relevant outcomes, often because they might be intangibles), patchy (not all relevant data-sets are generated or used in a uniform way across the country) and variable in quality or specificity (they might be on inappropriate geographical levels of aggregation).[1]

- Certain sectors, such as sports, have made consistent attempts to create 'outcome evidence frameworks', one example being Sport England's Evaluating Impact programme (see website for details). They have invested in these frameworks as multi-year programmes. Even so, the link between the evidence generated and policy influence is unclear or, indeed, might lead to an undesirable effect on the debate, as has been shown to be the case in the cultural sector.

Fundamentally these problems exist because when it comes to instrumental benefits, play, just like culture provision, creates a potential rather than predictable effect (Holden 2006). However, that does not mean that interesting avenues for further quantitative research could not be pursued.

Our research has shown that there is potential in further developing contingent valuation methods to elicit the willingness of respondents (typically parents) to pay for play provision as a (public) commodity without a clear market price (Atkinson and others 2006) – responses from parents to such methods generally seem positive. Also, there are

---

1   Even the new National Indicator Set measures data mostly at the level of local authorities rather than at the level of individual wards. The latter would be required before making claims about the impact of particular play provision sites as opposed to local authority standards in general (see National Indicators Set website, accessed 5 November 2008).

methodological developments in trying to measure capabilities, through policy intervention (Anand, Santos and Smith, 2009 forthcoming). Equally, there has been increasing research linking public-realm quality to house price, the methodology of which could be useful for establishing a link between play provision and house prices (CABE 2007). Some of these approaches could be combined with the emerging work led by Play England on local play indicators (Play England 2008).

Lastly, the evaluation of Play Pathfinder pilots, currently in development, offers a great opportunity to design ex-ante and ex-post evaluation schemes which build on the evidence base and further the discussion about necessary data-sets and methods of measurement (DCSF 2008). However, none of these are simple and clear cut, and none of them can rely exclusively on generating quantitative data without paying attention to the rich stories that children and parents themselves can tell us.

Image: Wansdyke Play Association

Great strides have been made, in recent years, in addressing the poor state of play for children and young people in this country and in creating perspectives for their improvement. Recent investment, through the Big Lottery Fund's Children's Play initiative and the government's Children's Plan and Play Strategy, has been much needed and welcome, and is the best evidence that parents, children and the play sector have been successful in making the case for play. The research in this study shows how this is making a difference on the ground – not just in terms of funding, but also in a fundamental change of tone and terms in policy debate, in a shared capacity to understand the issues facing young people and their rights, in the delivery by public sector agencies and in the benefit accruing to different agenda. The argument for investment in play provision is now becoming more widely accepted.

This report started with asserting that play provision should be judged by whether it enables children to play, first and foremost, rather than focusing on instrumental outcomes. It has shown not only a series of powerful narratives of how to do this, through staffed play provision, but also a widespread commitment to these aims across policy sectors. Key stakeholders are convinced that powerful benefits can be derived from play provision, from health through to community cohesion, but that any improvement starts with improving the intrinsic offer of play for play's sake.

Principles in practice: The software of play provision

The research presented here also shows that across our case studies, these opportunities to play freely are created and sustained not through investment in the 'hardware' of sites and equipment alone, but crucially through a carefully crafted set of social protocols and codes that turn physical spaces into places of opportunity for children to have a wide range of experiences. These ideas are at the very heart of play theory and practice: in the Playwork Principles' definition of the role of the playworker as one of facilitation, not control (Principle 3), and of the site itself as belonging to the children (Principle 5) (see Preface). It is the respect that staff have for the process of play, and the individual, freely led and intrinsically motivated activities of children playing, that characterises these sites.

The value of free play opportunities, and of access to a place and adults who respect this play, is vital and apparent to children – but not just to them. Again and again, parents and a raft of policy stakeholders told us about the value they saw in these sites, and how the opportunities to play are shaped by the people who work there. Therefore, we would assert that the current round of investment should include careful and considered investment in the 'software' that is shown to underpin the success of play provision. This is crucial if play provision is to make a real difference to children and young people, to their parents and to the community.

This does not mean that unstaffed play provision has no value. There is ample research to show that the opportunity to play on the street, on the doorstep and in the local park is crucial for children, and that too often this local physical environment lets them down. The Demos report *Seen and Heard* (Beunderman, Hannon and Bradwell 2007) shows how the public realm fails as a network and how this needs to be redressed – children's and parents' accounts, in this study, of their scepticism and anxiety towards what most public spaces offer are a powerful reminder of that. But even if this were to improve, through the increased taming of traffic and the creation of playable everyday spaces, the opportunities to play need to be intensified in certain environments that offer a greater amount of affordances, by investing in settings that encourage a greater diversity of play, social interaction and personal experiences. It is through investment in the full range of staffed play provision, from community play centres to adventure playgrounds and play ranger projects, that we can achieve this.

In turn, such increased intensity of play opportunity can lead to a range of wider benefits: it will bring parents into contact with each other; it can form a cornerstone of the local third sector and neighbourhood life; it can provide a crucial touchpoint for, and an interface between, children and families in need and service providers, whether voluntary or public. This is not the same as instrumentalising play – it is emphasising that staffed play provision at its best is necessarily embedded in a rich, local, social network.

Towards a public engagement

Our research also showed a great anxiety, on the part of many staff and other stakeholders, about ways of recording, accounting for, showing and communicating these benefits. The sector is concerned that the current funding largesse might not last forever, and that, unless beneficial outcomes for children, their parents and the community can be **proven**, the sector might soon be vulnerable to accusations of inefficacy and a lack of accountability. This is mostly translated as: 'These outcomes need to be **measured**'.

As we argue in the previous chapter, there are indeed ways of doing this. Methodologies exist, although they are complex and costly, and the availability of data is at best still patchy. Experience from elsewhere, such as the sports and culture sectors, shows that a programme of outcome and impact evaluation is possible, though only with significant investment over time and with no guarantee of success. Meanwhile, for the play sector, recording and showing that new investment is increasing both access and use – which is a precondition for measuring benefit and impact – is already a significant challenge. This, rather than the more complicated assessment of outcomes, now seems the more urgent quantitative measurement challenge for frontline practitioners – although it is inherently limited in conveying the richness and diversity of what goes on in these places.

More fundamentally, however, the sector needs to reflect about where public legitimacy really comes from. From the sector's long experience of self-explanation to funders and the public, we recognise the need for a language capable of reflecting, recognising and capturing the full range of value generated through play provision, one that can tell this story to a wider audience. Even if play is now in the fortunate position where its intrinsic as well as instrumental value is being recognised by politicians, the discussions in the cultural sector show that both an over-reliance on any one element of the I–I–I value triangle or an overemphasis on the concerns of any one of the P–P–P groups (see Chapter 5) will be detrimental to a properly functioning system. Legitimacy is not a fixed entity that can be obtained and maintained between a professional sector and political class – it is a **process** that needs to be sustained (Habermas 1975, Barker 2001). Crucially, this needs to happen in interaction with, and through being open and accountable to the general **public**.

At a fundamental level we therefore argue that a limited approach to setting policy goals and a narrow focus on funding for the sector will, in the long run, struggle to succeed in creating the deeper legitimacy that is required if the aspirations of play professionals and (currently) politicians are to be made real. Wider openness to the community, public accountability and widely shared legitimacy are preconditions for securing a larger, and more secure, place for play provision in our public life, and therefore in the priorities of democratically elected governments – especially in the context of changing economic circumstances and budget pressures.

Such legitimacy will depend on institutional innovation that engages the public in understanding the benefit of play and engages them in contributing to the creation of this value. In this context, the negative attitude to children and play in the public realm, which have often been identified as key obstacles to improvement, urgently need to be redressed (Beunderman, Hannon and Bradwell 2007). Encouragement of this change, by the full range of institutions and practitioners, should be the principal ambition for the play sector, and evidence from our six case studies shows that successful sites of play provision are already achieving it: when non-parent neighbours come and offer to cut the grass on an adventure playground, as is the case in GAPA, something interesting is happening.[2]

However, even the successful play providers studied in this research have indicated that they permanently face budget cuts and changes in funding programmes. This means that playwork staff face a perpetual insecurity stemming from short-term job contracts and the difficulties of maintaining third party relationships. In such a context,

2   However, were the adults then to be permitted to co-opt, or 'adulterate', the site and its provision, it would run the risk of failing the children in a fundamental way. This balance is a difficult one to strike, although our case studies demonstrate that finding it is a process that can benefit us all.

the drive to expand provision, such as through the Play Pathfinder programme, with its short timescale, could be in danger of diluting the quality and unique characteristics described above. This is a classic public service dilemma: how to preserve the quality and ethos that underpin the success of particular organisations whilst rolling out new provision at the same time. A typical example is the rapid scaling up of Sure Start after the success of an initial, carefully grown and smaller-scale programme. Valuable characteristics such as local ownership, community development and bottom-up management were lost under mounting pressure to increase output, leading some critics to argue that the programme was 'dismantled in everything but name' (*Guardian* 5 January 2005). The current expansion of staffed play provision should learn from this experience.

Overcoming these challenges requires a reinforced effort on the part of professionals in the frontline of the sector: redoubling outreach to increase access, and taking the powerful stories emerging from accounts, as in this report, out to the public at large, while taking responsibility as playworkers to engage in adult agenda without compromising the precedence of free play onsite (Playwork Principle 4). To do this, they will almost certainly need strategic support over and above what is currently being provided.

There might be a role for Play England here to point to existing good practice: powerful stories of children's play are already shared between practitioners as part of reflexive practice. They can be drawn out through child-led projects that provide children and young people with the chance to tell their stories, becoming, effectively, a different form of play. Children and young people, as demonstrated here, are the best raconteurs of their own experiences. These stories, when turned into DVDs, exhibitions, pamphlets and seminars, are a vital way of sharing information and experiences between practitioners and of communicating the unique benefits of these sites to a wider audience.

The pitfalls of not doing this are clear. As the Demos pamphlet *Cultural Value and the Crisis of Legitimacy* argues:

> *Cultural professionals have focused on satisfying the policy demands of their funders in an attempt to gain the same unquestioning support for culture that exists for health or education; but the truth is that politicians will never be able to give that support until there exists a more broadly based and better articulated democratic consensus.*
>
> (Holden 2006: 9)

The flipside of this is that, whilst recognising the links between successful play provision and other policy agenda, politicians need to steer clear of thinking of play provision projects as resources that can be **used** as proxies for achieving the government's aims. Instead, the need is to respect play providers as partners who bring invaluable knowledge and unique expertise to the shared project of creating a more vibrant, participative public realm and civic society with benefits that focus, first and foremost, on children's quality of life – which includes, in the Every Child Matters framework, enjoyment as well as developmental opportunities.

The challenge now is to enhance what has been called 'communities of participation', which offer the public the widest possible range of opportunities and settings in which to be involved. The civic infrastructure we describe in this report, and the active involvement it helps to foster in children, young people, their parents and the wider public, are essential to the realisation of this promise (Leadbeater 2008, 1997). These community contributors have different constitutions, forms and models of practice and behaviour – but they are all working towards outcomes that previously were in the sole domain of the state. How we harness, collate and communicate good practice and provide bridges for the exchange and dissemination of knowledge will become increasingly critical.

Recommendations

To do this in practice, the sector can build on the excellent work already carried out, such as that of the six play provision sites that formed part of this study. This points to an agenda that emphasises four elements:

1. Increasing outreach and accountability to strengthen legitimacy
2. Embedding 'software' in the funding regime and operational practice
3. The role of practitioners and their support infrastructure
4. An additional research agenda.

Increasing outreach and accountability to strengthen legitimacy

- Further increasing access and uptake of staffed play provision is the key challenge and may involve play staff being more explicit to parents about management style and the value and character of free play. This may also mean emphasising the diversity of particular activities on offer, whilst finding ways to engage parents in discussions around hot topics such as risk and privacy. The key here is to include adults in a dialogue based on principles of practice that workers feel confident rather than adjusting provision to suit community concerns.

- Existing play provision projects should actively seek to enhance their outreach to communities, for example by holding community open days, recording and communicating children's stories of enjoyment through play in creative ways, and working with elderly people through, say, oral history projects. Whilst of course the emphasis ought not to shift from the children's primacy of ownership, inviting others into the site can help dispel misconceptions about play spaces, particularly adventure playgrounds, which are often dismissed as 'messy' by outside adults.

- Opening up volunteering opportunities for members of the community beyond parents (e.g., in maintenance work) can be an important way of creating wider community links and could take on additional importance in a changing economic context where budget pressures and, potentially, rising local unemployment may necessitate new ways of creating and maintaining public value and social cohesion.

- Some play providers, although not all, still have a long way to go in terms of tracking output: some projects know how many children they reach, but many don't, and fewer still know how many children they do not reach even within their immediate locality, for example in the local ward(s). This is a necessary first step towards accountability and gauging impact, and towards widening access.

- Those in charge of the process of selecting sites and developing playgrounds need to learn from successfully developed, bottom-up community initiatives. These should be based on local energy, creativity and drive if they are to be sustainable. This might include the involvement of the public, through, for example, Citizen's Juries for the allocation of funding.

- Play provision sites should aim to have Friends groups to strengthen parent and non-parent involvement in running them, as well as to build capacity to fundraise and network with other third sector organisations.

- There should be strong encouragement for all play provision sites to work additionally in the wider public realm, through engaging in play ranger work and by linking up with other public institutions such as theatres and libraries.

- This additional work should be reflected in the further strengthening of organisational networks to include charities for the elderly, neighbourhood groups, and sustainable transport charities – both locally and nationally.

- The positive attitude that policy partners and stakeholders (such as the police) have of play should be capitalised upon through further capacity building and by enlisting them for advocacy among elected members and the wider public.

- Guidance in the development of play strategy already emphasises the involvement of the community and residents' associations, but notes that practices vary. Capacity building programmes need to strategically reinforce this element of community involvement in the writing and implementing of projects.

Embedding 'software' in the funding regime and operational practice

- At a strategic level, play programme and project funders need to recognise more explicitly the value of staff in play provision and invest in diversity, plurality, quality and community; this can involve working with schools as part of an extended offer, but not at the expense of other play settings.
- Funders need to be more concerned about sustainability, meaning less short-term project funding and greater attention paid (and budgets allocated) to building relationships and enabling staff to play their role.
- Evaluation should be about improving performance and investment in staff rather than being used merely as an advocacy tool to justify further funding.
- Entrepreneurialism of play provision organisations, such as linking up with the voluntary sector or public sector partners, needs to be encouraged and rewarded, although not at the expense of the allocation of the core budget.
- Fundamentally, there should be a new statutory obligation for local authorities to invest in the creation of play opportunity for all children and young people, unconstrained by the need to address other priorities of local government. There is a very real threat to play opportunity in the long term if this is not done.

The role of practitioners and their support infrastructure

- The success of the recommendations described above depends on the efforts of professional staff and volunteers, who often already see enhanced outreach and networking as a natural part of their work, and who (together with the children and young people themselves) are in the best position to communicate the stories and successes of play provision; they need to be further encouraged and rewarded for such roles.
- Within project and programme funding, resources need to be made available for such roles in an explicit manner. These include outreach to under-represented groups such as children from black and minority ethnic groups and those who are disabled.

- The roles of organisational networking and external communication will not come instinctively to every playworker, many of whom see their primary responsibility and motivation as working with children. This needs to be recognised and roles within play provider organisations differentiated.
- Whilst outcome measurement is met with scepticism within the sector and seen as an undesirable burden, an emphasis on outreach, increasing access and capturing success through stories will be more encouraging and acceptable to most professionals.
- Play England and other strategic organisations in the sector should recognise that it will be a challenge for many local organisations to capture and communicate their work confidently to the public. They need to work with local authorities to improve the support infrastructure and organisational capacity of play providers, especially those in the third sector.
- Policy-makers and funders should acknowledge the importance of the professional judgement of play staff. This recognition should enable them to extend beyond evidence-based decision-making.

Additional research agenda

- A new research and development agenda is needed which capitalises on the growing interest amongst policy-makers in the intrinsic benefits of play. One aspect of such research is to further emphasise the recording of access to, and uptake of, staffed and unstaffed play provision (in other words: output) as one of a range of methods to increase accountability.
- Another aspect of this agenda would be to focus on issues of organisational types and their differential capacity to outreach and network with partner and stakeholder organisations, set within a wider context of third sector capacity-building research.
- There is a need to obtain better insight into current public perception of (staffed) play provision in order to counter the negative attitude towards children and young people.

This is an agenda that will be challenging for the sector, but there are ample reasons for optimism. Many of the changes that are needed could come about in the context of current policy delivery, through an increased emphasis on the role of staff and community participation to set the atmosphere and culture for the new staffed play infrastructure.

It is crucial that the sector takes time to reflect and uses the opportunity brought about by the current policy and funding climate to forge new and sustainable relationships with the general public, embedding staffed play provision in the heart of neighbourhoods and community life. This will promote a strong play culture, confident in and communicative of its own worth, instead of a weak sector dedicated to the production of ancillary benefits. In this way the sector will simultaneously address the kinds of understanding, learning and development that are necessary for play professionals to fully meet the challenge laid out – that of engaging more directly with the public. Solutions are best generated by those people closest to the issues, rather than by outside commentators – especially in a field such as play, which deals with the issues and stories of young people in their everyday lives within their everyday environment, which is, inevitably, local, dynamic and particular.

References

Action for Sick Children Education pack (no date) 'Pictures of healthcare: A child's eye view'. Cited in: Creegan, C and others (2004), 20.

Amin, A (2002) 'The multicultural city: Living with ethnic diversity', *The Edge*, 10 July 2002. http://www.esrcsocietytoday.esrc.ac.uk/ESRCInfoCentre/about/CI/CP/the_edge/issue10/multicultural_2.aspx?ComponentId=10682&SourcePageId= 3446 (accessed 20 July 2007).

Amin, A (2007) Thinking Past Integration and Community Cohesion. Paper presented at 2007 COMPAS annual conference, Oxford University, 5–6 July 2007.

Anand, P, Santos, C and Smith, R (2008) 'The measurement of capabilities', in Basu, K and Kanbur, R (eds) *Arguments for a Better World: Essays in Honour of Amartya Sen*. Oxford: Oxford University Press.

Atkinson, G and others (eds) (2006) *Recent Developments in Cost–benefit Analysis for the Environment*. Paris: Organisation for Economic Co-operation and Development.

Bach, R (1993) *Changing Relations: Newcomers and established presidents in US communities*. New York: Ford Foundation. Quoted in: Vertovec, S (2007) *New Complexities of Cohesion in Britain: Super-diversity, Transnationalism and Civil-Integration*. Oxford: ESRC Centre on Migration, Policy and Society, 33.

Barker, R (2001) *Legitimating Identities: The self-presentations of rulers and subjects*. Cambridge: Cambridge University Press.

Barnett, LA (1990) 'Developmental benefits of play for children', *Journal of Leisure Research*, 22, 2, 38–153.

Barnett, LA and Storm, B (1981) 'Play, pleasure and pain: The reduction of anxiety through play', *Leisure Sciences*, 4, 2, 161–75.

Bartlett, J and Leadbeater, C (2008) *Making It Personal*. London: Demos.

BBC News (2006) 'The cost to parents of school', BBC News website, 16 August. http://news.bbc.co.uk/1/hi/education/4797497.stm

Beunderman, J and Lownsbrough, H (2007) *Equally Spaced? Public space and interaction between diverse communities*. Report for the Commission for Racial Equality. http://www.demos.co.uk/files/Equally%20Spaced.pdf (accessed 20 October 2008).

Beunderman, J, Hannon, C and Bradwell, P (2007) *Seen and Heard*. London: Demos/ Play England.

Bonel, P and Lindon, J (1996) *Good Practice in Playwork*. Cheltenham: Stanley Thornes, 14.

Bradwell, P, Hannon, C and Tims, C (2008) *Video Republic*. London: Demos.

British Heart Foundation (2000) *Couch Kids: The growing epidemic*. London: British Heart Foundation.

Brown, F (2006) 'Play Theories and the Value of Play', *Highlight*, 223.

Buonfino, A and Hilder, P (2006) *Neighbouring in Contemporary Britain*. A think-piece for the Joseph Rowntree Foundation Housing and Neighbourhoods Committee. York/London: Joseph Rowntree Foundation/Young Foundation.

CABE (2005) *Parks Need Parkforce*. London: Commission for Architecture and the Built Environment.

CABE (2007) *Paved With Gold: The real value of street design*. London: Commission for Architecture and the Built Environment.

Cale, L and Almond, L (1992) 'Children's activity levels: A review of studies conducted on British children', *Physical Education Review*, 15, 2, 111–18.

Children, Youth and Environments Center for Research and Design (2007) *Benefits of Nature for Children's Health*. Fact Sheet #1. Children, Youth and Environments Center for Research and Design, University of Colorado.

Children's Play Council, National Playing Fields Association and Playlink (2000) *Best Play: What play provision should do for children*. London: CPC.

Cleaner Safer Greener website. http://www.cleanersafergreener.gov.uk/ (accessed 4 November 2008).

Coalter, F and Taylor, J (2001) *Realising the Potential of Cultural Services: The case for play*. London: Local Government Association research briefing. http://www.lga.gov.uk/lga/aio/341747 (accessed 4 November 2008)

Cole-Hamilton, I and Gill, T (2002) *Making the Case for Play: Building policies and strategies for school-age children*. London: NCB.

Cole-Hamilton, I, Harrop, A and Street, C (2002) *Making the Case for Play: Gathering the evidence*. London: NCB.

Communities and Local Government (2008) *Communities in Control: Real people, real power*. CLG White Paper (accessed 4 November 2008).

Communities and Local Government website. http://www.communities.gov.uk/localgovernment/performanceframeworkpartnerships/nationalindicators/ (accessed 20 October 2008).

Craig, J and Skidmore, P (2005) *Start with People: How community organisations put citizens in the driving seat*. London: Demos.

Creegan, C and others (2004) *Evaluation of the Tower Hamlets Community Play Programme*. London: Barnardo's Policy and Research Unit.

DCSF (2007) *The Children's Plan: Building brighter futures*. London: Department for Children, Schools and Families.

DCSF (2008) *Analysis and Evidence Strategy*. London: Department for Children, Schools and Families.

DCSF (2008) *Fair Play: A consultation on the play strategy*. London: Department for Children, Schools and Families.

Department of Health (2004) *At Least Five a Week: Evidence on the impact of physical activity and its relationship to health*. London: Department of Health.

Department of Health (2008) *Healthy Weight, Healthy Lives: A cross-government research and surveillance plan for England*. London: Department of Health.

Every Child Matters website. http://www.everychildmatters.gov.uk/culturesportplay (accessed 4 November 2008).

Fisher, W (1987) *Human Communication as Narration: Toward a philosophy of reason, value and action*. Columbia, SC: University of South Carolina Press.

Foresight (2007) *Tackling Obesities: Future Choices – Project report*. London: Government Office for Science.

GLA (2008) 'Providing for children and young people's play and informal recreation'. Supplementary Planning Guidance for The London Plan. Greater London Authority, March 2008.

Glass, G (2005) 'Surely some mistake? The dismantling of SureStart projects' in *Guardian*, 5 January.

Good Childhood enquiry. http://www.childrenssociety.org.uk/all_about_us/how_we_do_it/the_good_childhood_inquiry/1818.html (accessed 10 October 2008)

Granovetter, M (1973) 'The strength of weak ties', *American Journal of Sociology*, 78, 6, May, 1360–80.

Habermas, J (1975) *Legitimation Crisis*. Boston: Beacon Press.

Harlow, HF and Suomi, SJ (1971) 'Social recovery by isolation-reared monkeys', *Proceedings of the National Academy of Science of the United States of America*, 68, 7, 1534–38.

Hassan, G, Mean, M and Tims, C (2007) *The Dreaming City: Glasgow 2020 and the power of mass imagination*. London: Demos.

Heapy, J and Parker, S (2005) *The Journey to the Interface*. London: Demos.

Holden, J (2004) *Capturing Cultural Value*. London: Demos.

Holden, J (2006) *Cultural Value and the Crisis of Legitimacy*. London: Demos.

Holden, J and Jones, S (2006) *Knowledge and Inspiration: The democratic face of culture*. London: Demos/The Museums, Libraries and Archives Council.

Hughes, B (2002) *A Playworker's Taxonomy of Play Types*. London: Playlink. Second edn.

The Sunday Independent 'Helping Children to Play Stunts Creativity', 4 December 2000. http://www.sundayindependent.co.za

Institute of Education homepage. http://www.ioe.ac.uk/schools/ecpe/eppe/index.htm (accessed 4 November 2008).

Kapasi, H (2006) *Neighbourhood Play and Community Action. Evaluation of the Neighbourhood Play Toolkit programme*. York: Joseph Rowntree Foundation.

Kelly, G. and others (2002) *Creating Public Value: An analytical framework for public service reform*. London: Cabinet Office.

Kuh, DJL and Cooper, C (1992) 'Physical activity at 36 years: Patterns and childhood predictors in a longitudinal study', *Journal of Epidemiology and Community Health*, 46, 114–19.

Leadbeater, C (1997) *The Rise of the Social Entrepreneur*. London: Demos.

Leadbeater, C (2008) *We-think: The power of mass creativity*. London: Profile Books.

Lester, S and Russell, W (2008) *Play for a Change – Play Policy and Practice: A review of contemporary perspectives*. London: Play England/NCB.

Mackett, R (2004) *Making Children's Lives More Active*. London: UCL Centre for Transport Studies.

Margo, J and others (2006) *Freedom's Orphans: Raising youth in a changing world*. London: Institute for Public Policy Research.

McKendrick, JH, Fielder, A and Bradford, MG (1999) 'Privatisation of collective play spaces in the United Kingdom', *Built Environment*, 25, 1, 44–57.

Moss, P and Petrie, P (2002) *Children's Services to Children's Spaces: Public policy, children and childhood*. New York: Routledge/Falmer.

National Indicators Set website. http://www.communities.gov.uk/localgovernment/performanceframeworkpartnerships/nationalindicators/ (accessed 5 November 2008)

New Policy Institute (2002) *The Value of Children's Play and Play Provision: A systemic review of the literature*. London: New Policy Institute.

Nussbaum, M (2000) *Women and Human Development: The Capabilities Approach*. Cambridge: Cambridge University Press.

Nussbaum, M and Sen, A (eds) (1993) *The Quality of Life*. Oxford: Clarendon Press.

Office for the Third Sector website. http://www.cabinetoffice.gov.uk/third_sector.aspx

Parker, S and Bartlett, J (2008) *Towards Agile Government*. Melbourne: Victoria State Services Authority.

Parker, S and others (2008) *State of Trust: How to build better relationships between councils and the public*. London: Demos.

Pellegrini, AD and Smith, PK (1998) 'The development of play during childhood: Forms and possible functions', *Child Psychology and Psychiatry Review*, 3, 2, 51–7.

Peñalosa, E and Ives, S (2002) 'The politics of happiness', *Yes!*. http://www.yesmagazine.org

Perkins, D and others (2004) 'Childhood and adolescent sports participation as predictors of participation in sports and physical fitness activities during young adulthood', *Youth Society*, 35, 495–520.

Play England (2007) *Charter for Children's Play* http://www.playengland.org.uk/resources/charter-for-childrens-play.pdf (accessed 15 January 2010).

Play England (2008) *Summary of Local Play Indicators*. http://www.playengland.org.uk/resources/local-play-indicators.pdf (accessed 5 November 2008)

Playwork Principles Scrutiny Group (2005) *Playwork Principles*. London: SkillsActive. http://www.skillsactive.com/playwork/principles (accessed 15 January 2010).

Santer J, Griffiths, C and Goodall, D (2007) *Free Play in Early Childhood*. London: NCB/Play England.

Sen, A (1979) 'Utilitarianism and welfarism', *Journal of Philosophy*, LXXVI, 463–89.

Sheffield Hallam University/Centre for Regional, Economic and Social Research (2006) *How is the NDC programme to be evaluated?* Sheffield: Sheffield Hallam University/CRESR.

Simmons, A (2006) *The Story Factor: Inspiration, influence and persuasion through the art of storytelling*. New York: Basic Books. Quoted in: Hassan, G, Mean, M and Tims, C (2007) *The Dreaming City: Glasgow 2020 and the power of mass imagination*. London: Demos.

Sport England (2006) 'Understanding the success factors in Sport Action Zones'. Sport England. http://www.sportengland.org

Sport England's Evaluating Impact programme at http://www.sportengland.org

Sturrock, G and Else, P (1998) 'The playground as therapeutic space: Playwork as healing' (known as 'The Colorado Paper'), in Sturrock, G and Else, P (2005) *Therapeutic Playwork Reader: One*. Sheffield: Ludemos.

Thames Valley Police (1999) *Youth Shelters and Sports Systems: A good practice guide*. Thames Valley Police.

Thomas, G and Thompson, G (2004) *A Child's Place*. London: Demos/ Green Alliance.

Thomas, S and Bradburne, J (2006) *Making Playful Learning Visible*. Slough: Next Generation Foundation.

Torbay Children's Fund Annual Report 2005/06.

UNICEF (2007) *Child Poverty in Perspective: An overview of child well-being in rich countries*. Innocenti Report Card 7. Florence: UNICEF Innocenti Research Centre.